Love Greater
Than Faith

Translated from the French
Original title: L'AMOUR PLUS GRAND QUE LA FOI

The Scripture quotations contained in this volume are from the New Revised Standard Version Bible, copyright © 1989 by the Division of Christian Education of the National Council of the Churches of Christ in the U.S.A., and are used by permission. All rights reserved.

© Copyright Prosveta S.A. 2001. All rights reserved for all countries. No part of this publication may be reproduced, translated, adapted, stored in a retrieval system or transmitted, whether privately or otherwise, in any form or by any means, electronic, mechanical, photocopying, audio-visual or otherwise, without the prior permission of author and publishers (Law of March 1957 revised).

Prosveta S.A – B.P.12 – 83601 Fréjus CEDEX (France)

ISSN 0763-2738
ISBN 2-85566-821-2
original edition: ISBN 2-85566-798-4

Omraam Mikhaël Aïvanhov

Love Greater Than Faith

Izvor Collection — No. 239

PROSVETA

TABLE OF CONTENTS

1. The uncertainties of modern man 9
2. Destructive doubt:
   Unification and bifurcation 21
3. Constructive doubt 35
4. 'Your faith has made you well' 55
5. Let it be done for you
   according to your appreciation 73
6. Only our actions witness to our faith .. 97
7. Never abandon your faith in good 115
8. 'Unless you become like children' 141
9. 'The greatest of these is love' 159
10. Base your trust on vigilance 185
11. 'As I have loved you' 201

Readers are asked to note that Omraam Mikhaël Aïvanhov's teaching was exclusively oral. This volume includes passages from several different lectures all dealing with the same theme.

Chapter One

THE UNCERTAINTIES OF MODERN MAN

If you listen to the conversations of men and women around you, to radio and television programs, or to public speeches you cannot help but be struck by the fact that in spite of the strong convictions often expressed – and which fluctuate considerably depending on circumstances – people today are not really certain of anything. They have many philosophical, religious, scientific, political, and artistic opinions, but they give the impression of never feeling quite sure that they are treading on firm ground. Why is this?

For hundreds and thousands of years, the progress of science and technology was very slow. New discoveries were made every now and then, but the means of diffusing them were very limited, and even when they eventually began to be known and used they did not really change people's view of the world. No scientific or technical discoveries could undermine the notions of God and creation instilled in them by a religion that was based on the literal interpretation of scripture. For this reason, even when their lives were devastated by disaster, human beings still had an intimate sense of being part of a well-defined world in which the ground under their feet was solid and safe. They were upheld by a few unshakable beliefs. However happy or unhappy they might be, however disastrous their circumstances, they saw no reason to question their conception of the order of the world.

With time, however, the pace of scientific discoveries gathered speed, and with these discoveries doubt began to creep in. During the 20th Century, particularly, a great number of scientific convictions were swept away and supplanted by others. In the fields of physics, astronomy, and biology, for instance, each generation seems to have called into question the attainments of their predecessors, and whenever a new theory modified the foundations of our understanding of humankind and the universe, our conception of the God who created human beings and the universe was also modified. Religion, to which human beings had always turned for answers to all their questions, could no longer give them what they needed. The rapid proliferation of discoveries and theories – there is no need to mention specifics, you all know them – have

The uncertainties of modern man

contributed to creating a climate of uncertainty so that today no one is sure of anything anymore. Since people are always expecting some new theory to turn up, they are less and less inclined to believe that any absolute truths exist. They say, 'Let's wait and see... there is more to come.' And this mentality is rapidly gaining ground in every domain.

This, then, is the source of the malaise of modern human beings: the world in which they live is no longer familiar to them. As they can be sure of nothing they drift in different directions, always looking for something, but with no clear idea of what they are looking for. Indeed, uncertainty has now gained science itself, the one area that seemed most secure, so what credence can anyone give to moral, religious, or spiritual notions which have no foundation in objective fact and which even conflict with scientific discoveries? Things are in a state of suspense, and in the absence of any certitudes, those who are not really satisfied by materialistic science and philosophy begin to take an interest in the many kinds of spirituality that exist, going from one to the other, guided only by their feelings. The predominant state of mind today is curiosity, the appetite for novelty: 'What else is there to discover?'

Of course, there is nothing wrong in showing interest and sympathy for all forms of spirituality.

It becomes dangerous only if you spread your interest too thin, if you never make up your mind to choose one method of work and stick to it. Please understand what I am saying: it is not a question of being Catholic, Protestant, Orthodox, Buddhist, Taoist, or none of the above. It is a question – and it concerns each one of us, believer and unbeliever alike – of adhering to a few essential spiritual truths and of putting them into practice. About this there can be no uncertainty.

Spirituality is not something that we are free to choose or not choose as with other disciplines such as sport, the languages, the arts, and so on. Given the way human beings are constructed, spirituality is a vital need, and as long as people refuse to acknowledge that need they will continue to engage in all kinds of activities that are not only absurd but also dangerous both for themselves and for others. Because of their nature, if they do not find the nourishment for which their souls and spirits clamor, they will be continually tormented by a sensation of inner emptiness and hunger which they will try in vain to satisfy.

A human being is a bottomless pit which can never be truly satisfied by material possessions, social success, pleasure, even great intellectual satisfaction. It should not surprise us, therefore, to see that so many extremely intelligent and gifted people end by falling into the worst kinds of

The uncertainties of modern man

aberration. Unable to find what they are looking for – unaware, even, that they are looking for something – they are caught up in an endless quest for ever more public exposure, more power, more money, more territory, more forms of pleasure, and to get these things they are ready to subjugate or destroy all who stand in their way. But even when they achieve the goal they lusted after, they are still not satisfied, for they never succeed in filling the void that is like a yawning chasm within them.

The only way to fill that void is to accept to live in uncertainty but with a spiritual ideal. A spiritual ideal links us to a higher world from which we receive nourishment. And those who have once tasted – if only for an instant – the elixir of divine life receive more than they can ever get from years of study, success, power, glory, or pleasure. Does this surprise you? If it does, it means that you do not understand the nature of the spiritual world. The spiritual world is concerned with quality, and this distinguishes it from the physical world, which is concerned with quantity. It is the quality of the life of your soul and spirit which can, in an instant, fulfil you in a way that no accumulation of material possessions could ever achieve.

There is no reason, therefore, to be so full of admiration for all the brilliant, opulent, powerful people who have no room in their lives for the soul and the spirit. Above all, you must never trust them. Since they are not looking for spiritual nourishment, the only kind that could satisfy them, they are like ravening beasts, and their ambition, their lust, their gluttony lead them inevitably into paths that are dangerous for themselves and those around them.

Unfortunately, many so-called spiritual people are no better. They want the same prizes as materialists, and in pursuit of them they use the means of initiatic science. This is why I say they are even more blameworthy than materialists, for they degrade the most sacred principles. They may be visibly satisfied and pleased with themselves for succeeding with these means, but heaven, which does not appreciate being used for selfish ends, will one day demand a reckoning, and their punishment will be very severe. The truth is that even though such people called themselves spiritualists they do not really have faith. The first concern of those who have faith is to avoid transgressing the divine laws, the laws of self-abnegation, love, and sacrifice.

The one thing that can give you true certainty is to realize that you are, each one of you, a spiritual entity whose life is linked to the universe and who can obtain whatever you desire in the infinite worlds of the soul and spirit. Once you understand this you will no longer need to pursue

The uncertainties of modern man

ephemeral satisfactions. So be on your guard! Even though social and material success may seem, more and more, to be the only security you have, you must at all costs avoid making it your first priority, for it would be the ruin of you. If you are offered an important position in a particular field because your competence has proved your worth, accept it if you wish, but take care not to abandon the only thing that matters. You are not on earth for the purpose of becoming a chief executive, employer, director, minister, or president. You are on earth in order to work within the sphere of matter to become a fully conscious son or daughter of God. This is the only certainty you need.

It is excellent to explore matter and work on it and with it in order to organize, embellish, and vivify it. I would be the first to counsel you not to abandon matter. But it is even more important to begin by vivifying, organizing, and embellishing your own inner matter, so as to feel yourself confident, free, and in peace. Once you have learned to work on yourself with the powers of the spirit, not only will you make certain discoveries, but all that you accomplish outwardly will bear the mark of the spirit, of the light, the love, and the power of the spirit.

Some philosophers, reflecting on the question of faith, have said that a little knowledge distances us from God, but more knowledge brings us closer to him. This is true, but only if it is understood that we are not talking about the same kind of knowledge. A little more knowledge in the domain of biology, chemistry, or astrophysics will not bring you closer to God, it may serve only to increase your sense of uncertainty. The kind of knowledge on which faith is based is quite different. It is a knowledge that concerns you yourself, by which I mean your deepest self with all its wealth, all its infinite possibilities.

If you are still looking outside yourself for what you need, it means that you do not really believe in the divine power that flows within you. In your subconscious mind there is no faith, only uncertainty. This is why you are still hungering and thirsting for something, still in a void. Faith has to reach down into the very roots of life. As long as you have not learned to draw on that inner source, you will continue to drift in different directions and will be an easy prey for charlatans and fake purveyors of healing and happiness. The true freedom of human beings lies in this God-given power to find all they need within themselves.

I shall never tire of repeating this truth to you, for the sole task of a genuine spiritual guide is to liberate human beings. Many people suppose that a spiritual Master is a despot who uses his powers to impose his convictions on others. Well, they are wrong; it is exactly the opposite. A spiritual Master

The uncertainties of modern man

has no desire to impose his own will or convictions on others, or rather, he has only one conviction to impose on them, the conviction that their salvation lies exclusively in themselves. After that, all he does is show them the methods to use and the experiences they need in order to get there.

You often hear me say, 'Believe me...', but that does not mean that I want you to trust me blindly. I am simply asking you to take what I tell you seriously, to meditate on it, to try it out and verify it for yourselves. For if you do so I am certain that you will believe me, whereas if you believe me blindly and without reflection, at some time or another anyone or anything could sway you. Contrary to what most people imagine, faith is not a blind, baseless belief. In fact, it is because they think this that they are still in the grip of uncertainty. Faith, like science, is based on verification, experience, and lucidity.

Chapter Two

DESTRUCTIVE DOUBT:
UNIFICATION AND BIFURCATION

Some people smile knowingly at the mention of the truths of spiritual science and say, 'Oh, you know, I'm a doubter, a skeptic...' as though their skepticism were the fruit of years of deep thought. In reality, their attitude only shows how intellectually limited they are. They have not studied, and they do not want to study so they find it convenient to assume an attitude which allows them to avoid any true reflection and give the illusion that they are great thinkers. Yes, those who claim to be skeptics are simply demonstrating that they have never studied anything in depth. Since they have acquired no certainty, it means that they have not pursued their research sufficiently to reach a conclusion. And it means, too, that they are conceited enough to see no value in what other people have learned.

Skeptics are like those self-acclaimed 'seekers after truth' who, at the age of sixty or seventy, say that in spite of their years of research they have still not found it. They continue to repeat this in their conversations, thinking in this way to prove how rigorous and critical they are when it comes to ideas. What great thinkers! The truth is that they are seeking nothing at all... or rather, they are seeking anything but truth, for if they had really looked for it they would have found it long ago. They are simply giving themselves a convenient pretext for doing no spiritual work.

A great many people continue to nourish this inner state of perpetual uncertainty. Those who assert that they do not believe are at least expressing some kind of conviction. But those who only doubt are forever being swayed this way and that. One day they lean toward one thing, the next day toward another, and when the time comes to act they keep putting it off: 'Should I commit myself in this way? Wouldn't it be better to do something else?' Such a situation is deplorable. It is legitimate to hesitate and question things before acting – in fact, it is useful to do so – but not to spend your whole life in a state of hesitation. A time comes when it is necessary to reach some form of certainty, to make a decision and act on it. Doubt dilutes your strength and disrupts your thoughts and feelings. And once your thoughts and feelings are disrupted, your will-power is weakened and it becomes impossible to muster the necessary effort.

Destructive doubt: Unification and bifurcation

Doubt paralyzes and divides. Jesus said: *'No house divided against itself will stand'*,[1] and of course we are all familiar with the phrase 'divide and reign'. You all know that the best way to weaken a group of people and impose your will on them is to introduce a division in their ranks. Isn't this a common enough sight? If your competence and personal qualities do not allow you to impose your will on a government, a business, any form of association, even a family, do you not instinctively seek to introduce division into the group?

But if the deadly effects of division in all forms of political, professional, social and familial associations are well known, their effects in the inner life have not been so closely studied. Those who doubt introduce division within themselves. It is as though they wanted to go two different ways at the same time, and the result is that they stagger between the two. You will object that it is not always easy to be certain what you should do. I know, but there is one way to avoid destructive doubt, and that is to raise your mind to a higher plane and tell yourself: 'I know I'm not perfect. I do not possess the intuition or the necessary lucidity to know the whole reality, but that should not worry or paralyze me. I put all my trust in good

---

[1] Mt 12:25

and in the light, and I'll continue to act with honesty, selflessness, and courage.'

If you are able to maintain this state of mind, you will always get the better of any doubts that beset you. Otherwise you will be like a tree that has been felled: how does the lumberjack split the trunk? Since he cannot do it simply with an axe, he does it by introducing a series of wedges into it. So draw your own conclusions: if you allow tiny wedges to be introduced into you every day, you will eventually be destroyed by all the blows that rain down on you and split you apart. As soon as a thought or a feeling begins to split your trunk, it gradually disperses all your psychic and spiritual energies and you end as a heap of fragments. And yet are there any who do not know the slogan 'Strength in union'? Oh, yes, everybody knows it, they even apply it, but rarely in instances where it is most needed.

The question of doubt and faith reaches far beyond the realm of religion. It touches every aspect of life and affects both believers and non-believers. Faith pulls together and unifies, whereas doubt divides, splits apart, and produces bifurcations. It is extremely important for you not to tolerate a state of bifurcation in which two contradictory thoughts or desires manifest at the

Destructive doubt: Unification and bifurcation

same time and tear you apart, leaving you distraught and crippled. To avoid this disruption you must create unity within yourself.

When you have inner unity it means that all the parts of the periphery are harmoniously linked to the center so as to maintain the balance necessary for the manifestation and conservation of life. Unity is the law of life: atoms, molecules, organs, members, individuals, countries, all beings must, on one level or another, converge toward a center. Everything must be firmly linked and cling to the center to avoid being swept away by adverse currents. In ourselves, we may call that center God, but it can also be a high ideal or a vocation. Those who fail to link themselves to the center by means of their thoughts, feelings, and actions create a state of bifurcation, which, even if it is only momentary, leads to disorder, conflict, and ruptures.

Bifurcation – or the state of being torn two ways – means to try to serve two masters at the same time: God and Mammon, the powers of the spirit and of heaven, and those of earth and of matter. Those who do this are like double agents who spy for their country, and at the same time, for the enemies of their country. They think that whichever way things turn out, their future will be assured. And in many businesses you will find individuals who serve both their employer and his competitors. This kind of thing is extremely damaging for both countries and businesses, but it is equally damaging for the persons concerned, for they run the risk of being rejected by both sides. In the spiritual life, bifurcation is a mortal danger, and unfortunately most human beings find themselves to a greater or a lesser degree in this state.

Every time you find yourself faced with a choice, therefore, reflect carefully and once the right way to go becomes clear, make up your mind and act. If you hesitate, thinking, 'Wouldn't it involve more effort than I'm prepared to make?' or, 'Wouldn't I be acting against my own interests, because so-and-so would despise me for it?' you will be opening the door to forces of darkness that will undermine you. On the psychic as on the physical plane every action entails consequences. Those who look for an excuse not to do what their good judgement or intuition advise end by losing both judgement and intuition. You will not continue to see the way ahead clearly for long if you always balk at taking it because of the difficulties it involves. Yes, this is what happens when you allow yourself to be torn two ways: you lose the ability to judge.

When you know what is right you must not shilly-shally. Of course, this does not mean that you have to dive into something head first and without discernment. But you must not allow indecision or contradictory tendencies to gain the

Destructive doubt: Unification and bifurcation

upper hand, otherwise you will be like an empty house with all kinds of squatters trying to get in to live at the owner's expense.

Sometimes, when householders have to go away for a while, they invite friends to stay and look after their house in their absence. This shows that in the physical world they know what to do, but it never occurs to them that precautions also need to be taken in their inner world. So, if you do not feel quite safe, take care to install tenants in all the rooms of your house – if only temporarily. Call your luminous friends of the invisible world and tell them, 'I'm afraid of all the undesirables that are trying to get in. Please come and live here for a while.' Eventually, you will not want these good, intelligent, watchful friends to leave. You will keep them with you for ever.

Indecisiveness always has deplorable consequences in the long run. As soon as you realize that you are beginning to slip into such a state, you must remedy the situation. The first thing to do is find the reason, for there is necessarily a reason for it. At some time or another you must have committed some fault, and now, of course, you do not know quite where you stand or what you should do. The only remedy is to link yourself to the center, to recreate your inner unity around some kind of beneficial activity, thus taking a specific direction.

Doubt makes all movement or progress impossible. Even the smallest doubt can paralyze you. Think of how you feel, for instance, if you begin to doubt a friend's sincerity. You no longer know how to interpret what he says and does; everything about him seems suspect; it is as though something in your mind and your heart began to crumble away. You will say that doubts are sometimes justified, for friends are not always faithful. That is true, of course, and I take that example because I am sure that you must all have experienced it and it can help you to understand what happens when you allow doubts to creep in about essentials: the foundations of your life, its meaning, and the direction you give it. Here, too, everything begins to crumble away.

Unity is a necessary condition without which no stability and no constructive activity is possible. As soon as you sense an inner wavering or dispersal, enter into yourself and try to reach the unique center of your being. One of the most effective ways to do this is to link yourself to the sun, for the sun is the center of our planetary system, and when you link with the sun you also link with your own center. All the different currents that enter you will become organized around that center, and whatever the circumstances you will have a sense of inner equilibrium that nothing can destroy.

Destructive doubt: Unification and bifurcation 31

Equilibrium! What is of greater importance for our physical and psychic life? Let us begin by talking about physical equilibrium. What would happen if we did not have the center that enables us to move our limbs and walk about without falling over? We find it perfectly natural to stand up, sit down, walk, lean to one side or the other, and yet it is so easy to lose one's balance and to fall. Balance, equilibrium, is a constant victory over contradictory forces, and that is why it is continually in danger. We need to learn to control those forces, and in order to do so we need to see the situation clearly and be watchful and determined. If we look to one side while walking forward we will find ourselves on the floor.

As I have often told you, I love to watch acrobats at the circus. Their difficult and dangerous moves illustrate so well the moves we too have to make in our psychic life. However naturally talented they may be, they have to practise for years and repeat the same exercises thousands of times. It is thanks to that long experience that they can now launch themselves into space and be sure of reaching and grasping the handhold waiting for them, or dance on a wire high above the ground, knowing that they will not fall.

And yet acrobats do sometimes have accidents. They have practised their dangerous leaps over and over again, and then one day they fall. Why?

Because they suddenly find themselves faced with conditions that they have never known before. On the physical or the psychic plane something totally unexpected has happened. Perhaps some event in the last few days has troubled them, or perhaps the conditions in which they had always worked and succeeded were suddenly less good and they have become less sure of themselves. This has been confirmed by acrobats who have survived such accidents. They say that they had a premonition, that they had sensed a lack of self-confidence. They did not always know why, but their state of mind was less harmonious as though a doubt had crept in, and since they no longer had faith in what they were doing an accident was inevitable. When you work without faith – which alone is capable of mobilizing and unifying all your energies – you are heading for a fall of one kind or another.

This law is valid for all aspects of our inner life. Doubt can also creep in and undermine our efforts when we undertake the long and exacting spiritual work of self-perfection. Faced with the immensity of the task, the great distance still before us, and the number of obstacles to be overcome, we sometimes wonder what kind of adventure we are embarked upon and whether we really have the qualities necessary to bring it to a successful conclusion. You will say, 'How right you are! We

Destructive doubt: Unification and bifurcation 33

know that feeling so well.' Yes, and if you understand what faith is you will also know that you must do all in your power to prevent doubt from stealing into you, for doubt is synonymous with destruction.

We are all liable at some point in life to have terrible doubts about ourselves, and these doubts can gradually destroy us. Personally, I often have doubts about myself, but I have a method to prevent them from destroying me. I renew my faith in the being that dwells within me, the Deity himself, for it is impossible to doubt a being that is all light, love, and power. Why not use the same method for yourselves?

Whatever reasons you may have for doubting yourself, there is only one way to prevent the poison of doubt from destroying you, and that is to be aware that an all-powerful, omniscient and all-loving being dwells within you, and that by linking yourself with him and leaning on him, you can rebuild everything. You fight cold with heat; you fight darkness with light; you fight doubt with faith, faith in the reality of the divine presence within you.

Many people, when they meet with failure, tell themselves: 'I'm incompetent, weak, poor, and stupid. I'm worthless.' Agreed! You may well be stupid and incompetent and all the rest, but you must not dwell on it. That would be dangerous.

When you experience a period of this kind, show a little intelligence and tell yourself: 'All right, I'm worthless! I know it. But there are rich, beautiful, and wise beings in the world, and I can link myself to them and benefit from their qualities and virtues.'

Yes, if you find it difficult to link yourself to the Deity, because he seems so far away and inaccessible, you can at least create a bond with all those great beings who have made their mark in history because of their nobility of character and their gifts. And of course, if you can, link yourself to God by becoming conscious that he is within you. Try at the same time to recall all the wonderful moments of peace, light, and inspiration that you have already experienced, for once experienced they cannot be wiped out. Cling to those moments and little by little faith will come back to you.

Faith will be no use to you – neither will doubt, for that matter – if you do not use these methods that enable you to put them where they belong. To doubt God is to doubt yourself, and to doubt yourself is to doubt God, and it is a grave fault. So never let the slightest doubt creep into you about the existence of the divine spark within you, for this is the truth: it truly dwells within you.

Chapter Three

CONSTRUCTIVE DOUBT

A great many men and women have told me about their difficulties and failures, and most of them did not understand why they had failed. They would ask: 'Why am I in this state? Why can't I pull myself out of it?' And do you know what I sometimes answer? I say: 'It's very simple: all your misfortunes come from having too much faith.' Then they look at me in astonishment and say: 'But what faith? You mean because I believe in God?' 'No, no. I'm not talking about your faith in God. If you truly believed in God you would certainly not be in your present state. No, it is in yourself that you have too much faith. You are too sure of your intelligence, your powers of reasoning and your calculations. That is the faith that has been your downfall. If you doubted yourself a little you would be more discerning and would not get yourself into such impossible situations. So, think about it a little...'

Doubt is like a destructive insect, a cankerworm which frets and destroys, but only when it occurs in those regions where it has no business, that is, in the higher regions of light and love. You must prevent it from entering these regions – or rid yourself of it if it sneaks in, just as some birds rid trees of harmful insects – for doubt, like these insects, are detrimental to spiritual growth.

Now, be sure to understand me correctly. When I say that someone has too much faith in himself, I mean that he has allowed himself to listen to the suggestions of his lower self. If he believed in his divine self he would always be enlightened and would not take the wrong path. I could equally have told him that he had doubted too much, that he had doubted his higher self. He put all his capital in a bank that was unsafe – his lower self – and it went broke... which was only to be expected, for the lower self always ends in bankruptcy. The true art of living is to know what to believe in and what to doubt.

Those who know how to use doubt will continue to rise and advance. There are so many domains in which human beings would do well to doubt a little instead of throwing themselves headlong into dangerous undertakings. They believe, for instance, that this man or that woman will bring them happiness, they believe in the power of money, in their lucky star... above all they

Constructive doubt

believe in the calculations of their own limited intelligence. Well, they would do better if they doubted.

Consider the different reactions people have. Take, for example, the case of a dishonest businessman who finds himself being prosecuted for malpractice. The fact that he is in the dock means that his enterprise failed, but how is he going to explain that failure to himself? He will tell himself that, unfortunately, he neglected to foresee every eventuality and that next time he will be more careful. It does not occur to him to call into question the propriety of what he did. After all, he reasons, since society lives by the law of the jungle and everybody pursues his own interests to the detriment of others, why should he have any scruples? The important thing is not to get caught.

That, more or less, is how people react when their fraudulent schemes fail. They are ready to admit that the methods they used were not foolproof but not to call into question the legitimacy of their actions. They firmly believe that since they are living in an unjust world they need have no scruples. Well, this argument may seem acceptable to some, but those who desire to make spiritual progress should reject it out of hand. We are never justified in doing wrong on the pretext that everyone else does the same. Instead, we should ask ourselves what exactly we are likely to gain by assuming this point of view or persisting in that attitude, and be ready to question sincerely our own motivations.

How many thoughts, desires, and activities are inspired by people's lower nature! And they rush to obey. Our lower nature never hesitates, never doubts... and is never idle. It is quite extraordinary to see how men and women defend their most selfish interests, and the arguments they use. They feel entirely justified in lying, swindling, scheming, or breaking up a family... until, of course, they are caught red-handed. But does that stop them? Do they learn from their failures and begin to understand that it is their convictions that have played them false? No, as I say, most of them do not. They are content to think about how to succeed next time. The only thing that is real for them is what they think and feel. There is no room for doubt. So they persist in their ways as though there were no laws beyond those dictated by their own convictions and desires.

And yet the only thing that should never be doubted is the existence of divine laws which must be obeyed, for if we transgress them we will be punished in one way or another. Some of you may say, 'What! Are you, like everyone else, trying to make us believe that God keeps an eye on us and that he will punish us for our faults?' No, God has made the laws, but it is not he who punishes us if

Constructive doubt

we fail to abide by them. That is the task of other beings, just as it is in human society.

A legislator makes the laws, but it is not he who watches people to see whether they obey them or not. There are officials designated for that task, and when they find law-breakers they bring them before the courts of law which condemn them. Well, it is exactly the same when it comes to the laws instituted by God – or rather, by cosmic intelligence. There will always be a court of law to find you guilty and punish you if you disobey them, and if it is not a court of the land it will be your own inner courts of justice, which are far more terrible. At the moment you may feel immune from the hand of the law, you may even feel proud of what you have done, but the day will come when you will no longer be able to evade your own inner tribunal, and it is then that you will understand the true nature of the divine laws.

The greatest defect of human beings – the biggest obstacle in the way of their evolution – is their deep-rooted belief in the infallibility of their own reasoning, their own point of view. They protect and cultivate and defend it. You will say: 'But everybody has this weakness.' Yes, this obstinate clinging to one's own way of feeling and understanding things is the most widespread of all human weaknesses. They behave as though there could be nothing better, nothing more true than their own opinions and beliefs. They never wonder what region of their being these beliefs spring from or why they have one particular conviction rather than another. They let themselves be swept away blindly. This is why the earth has become the theater of constant confrontations in which each individual tries to impose his own point of view born of his own self-interest, his lusts, his whims, or simply the mood of the moment. It is only after suffering great misfortunes that human beings are ready to admit that they have not always judged things correctly, that they have allowed themselves to be guided by despicable motives.

No other human failing gives rise to so much disappointment and misfortune as this determination to defend certain beliefs and points of view without testing their validity. People persist in thinking that they are right even when all sorts of events in their daily lives prove the opposite. How can they put up with such contradictions? It is the events of life that should show you if your view of things is correct and not your own imagination, tastes, or preferences. I have given you all the criteria you need to see this clearly, and the most important is this: before making up your mind about something, try to identify what it is in yourself that urges you to behave in one way rather than another.

Doubt, it is true, restricts, weakens and paralyzes. If you have a job to do, a project to launch

Constructive doubt

and carry through, you must brush aside every doubt or hesitation however trifling, otherwise, in spite of all your efforts, you will not be in a fit state of mind to do what needs to be done, still less to persevere. But before starting to act... Yes, that is when it is wise to doubt, to study, analyze, weigh the pros and cons, and ask advice until it is all quite clear. The blind trust with which some people launch into action can only end in failure. If you refuse to see the reality that is all around you, if you refuse to take into account all the elements of a situation, you cannot help but fall on your face. Faith is one thing but obstinacy is quite another.

So many enterprises have failed in spite of the absolute confidence of those who undertook them. They may have lacked experience or failed to study sufficiently all the different aspects of the question beforehand. They imagined that all that was needed for success was to be motivated by the best possible intentions and to have confidence. No, that is not enough. This is the mistake of so many of those who claim to be working for an ideal: they are convinced that heaven will uphold them in all they do. Mountains of difficulties stand in their way, but they cannot – or will not – see them. They set out blindly, persuaded that God will be so pleased with their plans that he will smooth away those mountains. After all, does Isaiah not say: *'Thus says the Lord... I will go before you and level the mountains'?* [2] Well, no. It is not like that. The Almighty does not level mountains for those who are unwise and presumptuous. Let this be very clear to you.

The one thing God can do – the only thing you should ask him for therefore – is to give you the light you need. For the light will enable you to find the best way, to avoid pitfalls and precipices. It will give you the strength to carry your enterprise through to the end. Until you understand this even your best plans will fall through and you will run the risk of losing your faith. So many people say, 'Well, as God does not help me even though I am at his service, that's the end. I give up!' God does help them... but he cannot do anything for those who refuse to think before acting. And to think means to be a little doubtful of your capacity to see clearly and judge things entirely on your own. Without that initial doubt faith can lead to disaster. But once doubt has done its work it must be driven out without mercy. Once you have made up your mind in full knowledge of the facts you must not waver.

Thus doubt is the faculty that urges us to examine things more closely in order to understand them better and to act more efficiently. And it is thanks to this kind of doubt that you will one day

---

[2] Is 45:2

Constructive doubt

have cause to say that you have faith. Yes, it is by doubting that we strengthen and deepen our faith; by not being too sure of the rightness of our convictions, by doing our best to repulse every thought and feeling that might oppose the principles of true faith. For in reality true faith is knowledge.

Cosmic intelligence has done everything with great wisdom, and since it has given human beings the faculty of doubt, it is obviously in order that they may use it. The only question is where and when to use it. We should begin by doubting our capacity to understand and judge things correctly. You may say that this is difficult and you do not know where to begin. Yes, of course it is difficult, but there are signs that warn us when vigilance is needed. As soon as you sense a malaise, a certain hesitancy, you should see it as a sign that something is not quite right, and instead of clinging obstinately to your ideas, make use of this very effective tool of doubt. But use it correctly. Question the way you look at things, the way you habitually react to events, the methods you have used or intend to use. Tell yourself: 'Maybe I do not see things clearly enough. I still do not have all the elements I need to make up my mind. I still need to study the situation before I can be sure that my plans are consistent with the criteria of wisdom and love.' Never be content simply to accept whatever corresponds only to your point of view.

How many, do you think, would listen even to God himself if he came and told them something that was contrary to their own opinions and wishes? Most people would reply: 'No, no, Lord. You are wrong and I'm right. Listen...' And God would have to listen patiently to their explanations, justifications, and demands. Besides, are not most people's prayers just that? God is there to pay attention to their opinions and desires, and if any answer is expected of him, it is only: 'Yes, of course, my child. You're right. I will give you what you want.'

We all come into the world with our own psychic configuration which inclines us to prefer certain opinions and tastes rather than others, and to behave in certain ways. This is natural and normal. But we also come into the world with faculties of judgement and reason which enable us to accept or reject these natural inclinations. Instead of simply obeying your impulses, you should at least tell yourselves: 'Well I see and feel things in one way, but perhaps there are people who have studied things far longer than I and who are better informed. So all I can say at the moment is that I too will study the question more...' Stop saying: 'For my part, I think this... or believe that...', in the

Constructive doubt

assurance that you are right, for even if your point of view is justified there is always room for improvement. Yes, both your judgement and your behavior can always be improved upon.

The great thing is to find the happy mean between the doubt that paralyzes and that which liberates. It may be very useful for someone to feel that he is not sure of himself, if only because that may help him to improve his relations with others. People who are too sure of themselves irritate others and make enemies and have to spend their time quarrelling and settling scores. A little less self-assurance could be a protective measure, for it would help them not to go too far. They should tell themselves that they are neither very wise, nor very virtuous, nor very strong, and they would do well to trust only the one who is omniscient, omnipotent and all-loving. In this way, thanks to their self-doubt and their faith in God, they would make it possible for the Almighty to dwell in them and manifest through them, and wherever they went they would be a factor for peace and harmony.

It is always good to doubt oneself a little and to tell God: 'I know that I'm feeble, ignorant, and selfish, but I love you, my God. I believe in you and hope in you and ask you to manifest through me.' And because you show humility God will manifest through you, and you will receive true power, spiritual power. Your salvation lies in being conscious of your own insignificance and of the fact that your only greatness comes from God. There is nothing wrong in trusting in yourself, as long as through yourself it is in God that you trust, for only he is deserving of that trust.

Henceforth, whenever you are too sure of yourself and your opinions or of decisions you are about to make, try to introduce a little doubt into your mind. It will help you to avoid making too many blunders. Yes, a little self-doubt, a little self-examination can often be very useful. And let me add that it is those who are already materially and socially most successful who should be most careful. Having obtained money and power they have a tendency to believe that these are sufficient justification for their behavior. Since they have been so successful it must mean that they were right, and they can continue to impose their views, to contradict others, to decide things their way. What an illusion! The reality is simply that success has gone to their heads. This is why I give this warning to all those who imagine that their material success is proof of their good judgement. If they armed themselves with a little doubt they would be nearer the truth.

Yes, all those who are so proud of their determination would do well to be a little more prudent – and those who admire them also. They

Constructive doubt

gaze at them and exclaim: 'It's extraordinary! Such activity; such energy! Nothing deters them...' Such people are sometimes said to 'have no doubts.' But to have no doubts is no proof of the virtue of faith; it is rather proof of a presumptuous rashness. And not only do the presumptuous end by taking a fall, but – as history has shown us time and again – they also drag others down with them.

You have to be capable of obstinacy, but only after a careful examination of the underlying motives for your actions, only after making sure that you are on the right path. In spite of the difficulties that have to be faced at the beginning of a venture, all obstacles eventually disappear for those who are obstinate for good. Whereas although those who have never studied the true nature of their schemes and who persist in their error may seem to succeed, their success will not last: sooner or later the bubble will burst. To all of you I would like to say: 'Doubt the things of which you are most sure!' Yes, I preach doubt... Above all, if someone makes you a dazzling offer, then, more than at any other time, should you doubt. When you are offered money, honors, power, or pleasure... doubt.

In the Gospels we see that Jesus gave us an example of this kind of doubt. After he had fasted for forty days in the desert he was tempted by the devil. Satan said to him: 'You are hungry. Why don't you change those stones into bread? ... Throw yourself down from the temple; God will send angels to protect you... Look at all those kingdoms: I can give them to you...'[3] But Jesus rejected all the devil's suggestions because he knew what he should believe in and what he should doubt. He weighed the material benefits and compared them with the spiritual benefits, and he chose the spiritual benefits.

What can we learn from the example Jesus gave us? To make it clearer, let me give you a little exercise which consists of comparing two points of view. You all know at least one person, living or dead, who has manifested great wisdom, who understands things on a higher level. Now, every time a question comes up, ask yourself: 'My reaction is thus and so, but how would he or she react in my place?' By constantly making this comparison between yourself and that person, you will learn to adjust and correct your attitude.

Human beings have an instinctive tendency to compare themselves with others. Usually they do so in the hope of being able to point out how much better, more honest, or more intelligent they are than anyone else. Are such comparisons useful? Not very. It is not with ordinary, mediocre people that you should compare yourself, but with those

---

[3] Mt 4:1-11

Constructive doubt

who are more advanced. And history is full of examples of superior beings who, if we study their lives, can give us a true yardstick by which to measure ourselves. If we want to evolve it is with such as these that we should compare ourselves.

To compare is such a natural tendency that, although they do not realize it, human beings do nothing else. All their opinions and judgements about people and things are based on comparison. They prefer this person or this thing to that... Yes, but you cannot determine a preference unless you have first made some kind of comparison. Our judgement, the faculty that enables us to choose the path we take in life, is the result of the comparisons we are always making. This is why nature has placed the center of comparison in the center of the brain. The ability to compare is a quality that comes from Saturn – but from Saturn in its higher manifestations.

To compare, therefore, is an instinctive tendency. Look at children: even when they are very small they compare before choosing. Put a basket of apples in front of a child and it will immediately pick the biggest and the reddest. And they compare their toys and their clothes with those of their playmates. And this continues all their life. All their life human beings compare one house with another, one car with another, one social rank with another, and they try constantly to do as well as those who have more or more beautiful possessions and whom they believe to be happier.

On the material plane human beings are very good at making comparisons. But they are far less inclined to do the same for the things of the spirit. When they meet someone who is totally selfless and full of love, and who has acquired perfect mastery of himself, they do not ask themselves: 'What am I compared with him?' No, their need to compare is restricted to physical appearances, to things such as success, wealth, social rank, or power. Well, such a mentality makes progress impossible. If you want to advance you must compare yourselves with Jesus, with all the great Masters of humanity. Ask yourselves: 'How can I understand things as they do? I believe or feel this or that, but what about them? How do they feel? I wonder if they could not teach me to think and behave better.' Yes, that is constructive doubt.

All that I tell you is based on the principles of eternal wisdom. It is perfectly excusable if some of you do not fully understand, but to pronounce judgement without first studying it is simply presumptuous. The poor things who declare: 'According to me that is false... in my opinion that's just stupid...' are exposing themselves to real danger. What knowledge do they have that entitles them to say: 'In my opinion...'? As though their little 'me' possessed absolute truth! What pride!

Constructive doubt

Could they not be a little less conceited? When they have learned what others so much more advanced than they have said and done, when they have studied and experienced all the same things, then yes, they will be entitled to say 'According to me...' But not before. Of course, you cannot stop people speaking like this. Why shouldn't they? Everybody does it. True, but by speaking in this way they label themselves as presumptuous and ignorant.

We should study the virtues of doubt just as alchemists study the virtues of every kind of vegetable and mineral substance – even those that are poisonous – in order to learn how to use them. And now another example: when you are faced with a difficulty of some kind or when you hear some bad news, observe your own reactions. You will see that a mechanism is triggered within which makes you begin to worry, and the problem which was no bigger than a pebble ends by becoming an enormous obstacle in your path. Would it not be wiser to say: 'Wait; it may not be so bad. Things will probably sort themselves out.' In this way, instead of becoming an insuperable difficulty, the problem will fade away to almost nothing. But here too, instead of doubting, you are sure not only that it is evil but also that it will become worse.

No, it is evil that you must doubt. Stop saying: 'Oh, what a world we live in! People become more and more selfish and dishonest every day. They'll never change. Injustice always has the upper hand. Whatever we do to improve the situation, we'll never succeed.' Human beings are so attached to expressions like this that they are always inviting such thoughts to enter and dine with them... 'Come, come, there's plenty of food here for you.' Well, this is a very dangerous attitude. By emphasizing evil so much you do nothing to lessen it; on the contrary, you encourage and reinforce it.

From now on, therefore, you must encourage the good side of things. Say: 'O angels, come; heavenly entities, come; bring us your wisdom, love, and power so that we may be able every day to give something good to this world.' Yes, believe in goodness and doubt evil. This is the beginning of divine magic, of theurgy. Both white and black magic are based on doubt and on faith. A black magician doubts divine power and relies on the efficacy of the forces of darkness. A white magician or theurgist believes only in the forces of light, and it is the white magician that will have the final victory.

Chapter Four

'YOUR FAITH HAS MADE YOU WELL'

Most believers think that a spiritual Master is someone with great psychic powers which he can use anywhere and everywhere, whatever the conditions and whoever he may be with. Well, this is not the case, and I will prove it to you.

A passage in the Gospels tells us that when Jesus went to Nazareth he taught in the synagogue and the people distrusted him deeply. The passage concludes with these words: *And he did not do many deeds of power there, because of their unbelief.* [4] From this we can see that although Jesus possessed immense powers he did not manifest them when he was with people who did not believe in him. We also learn that when someone asked him to heal him or his child he replied: *'Let it be done to you according to your faith.'* and, *'Go, your faith has made you well.'* [5] Of course, those who

---

[4] Mt 13:58
[5] Mk 10:52

know no better will explain this by saying that Jesus was so vain and sensitive that he would help only those who believed in him blindly. No, the true reason is that faith is composed of subtle elements which facilitate manifestation, whereas doubt is composed of elements which make it impossible.

Jesus needed the faith of those who asked to be healed because faith is a necessary condition: it opens doors and windows and allows forces from other regions to enter a person and by entering to harmonize, purify, and regenerate the matter of his being. Jesus was a receptacle of divine energy, and it was this energy that he communicated to the men and women who asked him for help. You could say that those who went to Jesus asking for healing triggered a process as a result of which his power was made manifest. So you see, the miracles worked by Jesus – or what are said to be miracles, for in fact, miracles as most people understand them do not exist – implied that three conditions had been fulfilled.

For more than two thousand years the Church has been telling Christians that they must have faith, that faith alone can save them... and they have had faith. But as they have lacked true knowledge their faith did not do them much good, and they ended by losing it. Do you have faith? If you do well and good, but your faith has done no

'Your faith has made you well'

more than open a door, and if you have not set any process in motion by calling for help, nothing will happen, because nothing – no being, no forces – will enter by that door. It is essential to understand this clearly. Many Christians, relying on the fact that Jesus said *'Let it be done to you according to your faith'* and, *'Go, your faith has made you well.'* draw the conclusion that it is faith that heals, faith that works miracles. No, faith does not heal. It can assist the healing process but it does not perform miracles – at least, not in the way that this is generally understood. That which we call a miracle is the result of a force other than faith.

But what are people usually talking about when they speak of miracles? They are talking about extraordinary phenomena which defy or negate the laws of nature. Well, no such phenomena exist. If people speak of miracles, it is because they do not know the laws that would explain them. In reality, no manifestation can occur that is not governed by the laws of physics and chemistry. There can be phenomena that are exceptional because the beings capable of producing them are exceptional. But miracles such as pictured in the imagination of most believers simply do not exist. Even things that are truly extraordinary are natural. Nothing is 'supernatural'. But there are different levels or degrees in nature, from the most densely material to the most subtle. The laws of the psychic and spiritual worlds are laws of nature and the important thing is to know on what level they function.

If Jesus could heal the sick it was because he possessed the spiritual powers that enabled him to reach the causal plane and trigger a force on that plane which was capable of opposing sickness. But how many human beings ever possess this power? When people, claiming that faith heals, treat the sick by means of magic formulas, prayers, magnetism, or the laying on of hands they may trigger some slight improvement in conditions that are not serious, but they can do no more than that. However great their faith and that of their patients it is not enough. To be able to heal as Jesus healed, you not only have to possess the power of the spirit but also to have had long practice working with thought, the instrument of the spirit. And not everyone is capable of this either, for here again it is not enough to believe in the power of thought, you must first possess that power and have learned to master it.

Many sick people, having been disappointed by the shortcomings of medical science or alarmed by its increasingly materialistic tendencies, hope to find healing in spiritual practices that utilize the powers of thought. This is good. But here again you must be quite clear about what is involved. There are physical illnesses and there are psychic illnesses, and as our physical body and our psyche are not cut off from each other they obviously influence each other. Yes, but you must not mix things up: if you want results it is necessary to know where each element belongs.

Thought is an effective instrument for the reparation of damage on the psychic plane, but not on the physical plane. Results may not be seen very rapidly, but those who are capable of working with thought will end by overcoming sorrow, worry, and anguish. But to be able to influence the physical plane is quite another matter. For this you have to be capable of materializing your thought, and this requires exceptional powers and an exceptional degree of knowledge. Thought can affect matter only if it is highly concentrated and condensed, and those who want to use their thoughts to heal their own or other people's bodies before having achieved this will be laying themselves open to great disappointment. So many people have come and told me that they had tried to heal themselves through concentration and visualization and had achieved nothing. Well, it was only to be expected. Before being capable of healing through the powers of thought you have to have worked for a very long time on the intermediaries between the mental and the psychic planes, and in the meantime you have to accept that physical illnesses can be treated effectively only by physical means.

Of course, to have faith means to believe in the power of the spirit over matter. There is no going back on that. To the extent that the psychic influences the physical, it is possible to heal yourself by means of faith, but here too faith is not enough. It is no good believing and waiting for healing to fall from heaven. Faith has to be accompanied by genuine psychic work. Certain disorders – headaches, stomachache, or bilious attacks, for example – which are often caused by psychic upsets such as anger, anxiety, or despair, can be cured by the powers of thought. But as a general rule a physical illness must be treated by physical means.

Since it is impossible for most people to heal themselves by means of thought, the sensible course is to consult a doctor from the beginning and not wait until the illness has become incurable. But even those who are capable of influencing their health by means of thought should have recourse to medical treatment, for the development of an illness might well be more rapid than the effects of their mental work. Of course, if you have the patience to wait in order to see what the effects of thought can be, you can restrict yourself to working mentally. If your illness is not serious and if it develops very slowly, it will certainly give way in the end. But if it is something serious which develops rapidly, you must get medical treatment

'Your faith has made you well' 63

for it at once. If necessary, you should be ready to undergo surgery. It all depends on the type of illness.

Now, there is something essential that remains to be said, and it is this: a cure obtained by physical means may not be permanent. Why is this? Because an organic problem is very often the materialization of a psychic problem, of chaotic, poorly controlled thoughts and feelings. In order to recover your health therefore you will have to find and remedy the cause on the psychic plane. However, even if you manage to do this, it will take time for your work to produce results on the physical plane, and although the improvement obtained by physical means will not be lasting, it is necessary to have recourse to those means if only to gain a temporary respite from the ravages of illness. To combat a disease that has already damaged your physical body, you must use physical means, ranging from drugs to surgery. Your faith must not be a pretext to justify an irresponsible attitude toward your health. In this respect, we have to admit, materialists often behave more sensibly than spiritual people.

On the other hand, materialists also need to make progress in this area. They need to understand that the remedies that are so effective in the short term are often no more than palliatives. It makes sense to treat physical illnesses by physical means, but as I have just explained, this is often not enough. To the extent to which an illness is caused by past errors on the level of thoughts and feelings, it will always recur if no healing is effected on that level. The only solution is for those who are sick to use all the resources of medical science, and at the same time to correct the anomalies of their mental and emotional attitudes and thus eradicate the cause of their illness. Take the prescribed drugs; follow the prescribed treatment; but work mentally at the same time, for in the long run thought can affect matter and play a part in transforming it. This is true medical science. Take medicines if you have to, but add to them the power of your thoughts and of your faith, and they will be all the more effective.

To get the best results you need to find the right balance between the material and the spiritual. Solutions from outside ourselves are always inadequate, but since human beings are not yet capable of mastering their own inner world and of developing to the full all the powers of thought, they still need to combine the two, the inner and the outer. This means that doctors also have something to learn in this respect. When doctors prescribe a remedy, do they tell their patients that their attitude toward it can affect its efficacy? No, they do not. They behave as though the person

'Your faith has made you well' 65

were simply a body, a material organism which can be affected only by material elements, or worse yet, as though he or she were an automobile which only needed some gasoline in order to run properly. And yet doctors know that the psyche can influence the physical body. It is just that they are not in the habit of applying that knowledge – except in exceptional cases for which they prescribe a placebo.

We can certainly be glad of the tremendous strides made by medical science in the last few decades, but one of the results of this progress is that both patients and doctors now have recourse only to drugs or surgery, and they forget that mental work can contribute to the healing process. This reaction is exactly that of people who let themselves become physically and mentally slothful on the pretext that there are all kinds of machines that make effort unnecessary and can do their work for them. Think of all the movements, all the work you no longer have to do now that there are automobiles, machines to wash your clothes or your dishes, vacuum cleaners, remote controls, and so on. Of course, I approve of this progress, but only as long as it does not cause people to lose all sense of effort. If human beings are to develop correctly it is indispensable that they make efforts, both on the physical and especially on the psychic plane. Inactivity and laziness in whatever area are an obstacle to harmonious development.

Doctors have a great responsibility toward their patients. Not only must they know their speciality well in order to be able to diagnose and combat an illness, but their attitude toward their patients, the way they talk to them are extremely important. Their attitude and their words touch on a psychic factor in a patient, and you never know what positive or negative reactions they will elicit or the repercussions they will have on the patient's condition. It is very unwise for a doctor to tell a patient: 'You have three months... or six months to live'. First, because there is no guarantee that he is right; experience has so often shown doctors to be very wide of the mark in making such predictions. But also because it has a very negative effect on the patient, who is liable to give in to despair and be paralyzed by the conviction that nothing more can be done. You may say that, on the contrary, you have known sick people who were stimulated to react and fight against their disease when they heard this. That is possible, of course, anything is possible, but it is certainly not true for the majority.

Good doctors, who are aware that their patients are not simply machines which need to be repaired, give them the treatment they need, but at the same

'Your faith has made you well'   67

time they give them certain rules to respect and certain methods and exercises to help them recover inner equilibrium, peace, and harmony, saying: 'If you apply these methods you will live for a long time still.' In this way they give them the means to get well, and even if those means prove inadequate, at least the patients will have passed the time remaining to them in beneficial activities. And it is this that is essential: always to have a useful activity to which to devote oneself, for everything we do has consequences, if not on the physical plane, at least on the psychic and spiritual planes.

Many years ago in Paris I knew a man of about fifty who was completely paralyzed. He had been bedridden for more than a year and his doctors had declared him incurable. They said that only a miracle could save him, and his family as well as his doctor asked me to try to help him. I went to visit him, and I told him: 'Apparently medical science can do no more for you, but I will give you some methods, and if you apply them exactly as I say, you will be walking within two months. Do you believe me?' He said that he believed. The doctor and members of his family who were present also said that they trusted me, although their expressions seemed to indicate that they thought I had taken leave of my senses... Anyway,

I explained certain rules to him and told him what exercises to do each day. He did everything I told him with absolute trust, and effectively, two months later he was walking.

Nothing is possible without faith. I have often seen this in people I have tried to help. But faith is not enough. It is no good believing and waiting for a miracle to happen. Since so-called miracles are, in reality, a natural process, human beings can, by working inwardly as well as by physical exercises, participate in the healing process. You do not need me to explain what physical exercises to do, but what you do need is more light on the question of the inner work that has to be done.

If you want to act effectively on your physical body by means of thought, you must begin by setting in motion a particular form of energy, and as this energy comes from a very high plane, your first effort must be to raise your thoughts to the causal plane, that is, the higher mental plane. Mental work does not consist in repeating, 'I am getting better... my headaches will stop... no more bilious attacks...'. Neither does it consist in asking Jesus, the Virgin Mary, and all the saints to heal you. Of course, it is better to do that than to think of nothing but your ills, to moan and groan and be a nuisance to everyone else. But you can obtain true mental power over your physical body only by rising far higher than the astral plane of feelings,

'Your faith has made you well'

higher even than the mental plane of ordinary thoughts, in order to reach the causal plane. This is the explanation of certain cures reputed to be miraculous.

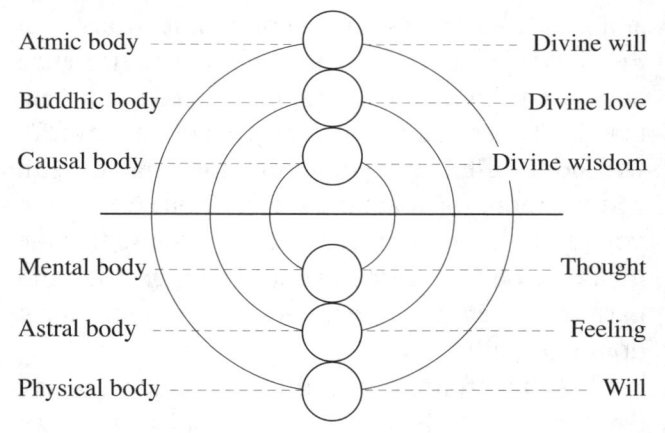

Atmic body	Divine will
Buddhic body	Divine love
Causal body	Divine wisdom
Mental body	Thought
Astral body	Feeling
Physical body	Will

I have sometimes been asked about the cures that take place at Lourdes. Well, of course, faith must have a large part to play in them, but some people must certainly be so uplifted, so carried away by the hymns and prayers and the great fervor of the crowds, that they actually attain the causal plane. It is this that produces miracles. People are raised inwardly above the ordinary level of consciousness to the highest levels of being, and when they reach those heights, powerful currents of the purest energy are set in motion within them and flow down through their being to the physical plane, and their health is restored.

But forget about exceptional cases of this kind. Not everyone makes the pilgrimage to Lourdes or elsewhere, but all are capable of practising this mental work every day at home in order to rise to a higher level and establish communications with the causal plane. Here again we see the difference between faith and a simple belief. You will find that the higher you rise inwardly the more powerful will be the elements you come into contact with and the more far-reaching their action. And when you reach the summit, God, you will sense that the idea of God is capable of establishing order and harmony in every dimension of your being, for it dominates all that is.

Yes, it is from the summit that you have power over the lower levels. No physical illness, no psychic anomaly however grave, none of this is incurable; there is nothing that cannot be remedied, but you have to rise to the summit. This is an essential truth discovered by the great spiritual Masters of humanity. When they need a solution for a problem, when they have questions that need to be answered, they always address the power of which Hermes Trismegistus said: 'As all things were by the contemplation of one, so all things arose from this one thing by a single act of adaptation.' It is this 'one thing', this cosmic power, that is God. Whatever your needs, it is to this one thing that you must try to rise, for it alone possesses all the elements capable of transforming and regenerating everything within you.

Chapter Five

LET IT BE DONE FOR YOU ACCORDING TO YOUR APPRECIATION

To the men and women who went to him and asked for help Jesus often replied: *'Let it be done for you according to your faith.'*[6] If we want to understand all that this means, we must give to the word 'faith' the broadest possible interpretation. For most people, to have faith means not only to believe in God but also to believe certain doctrines and dogmas formulated and taught by a Church, but for Jesus the word means far more than that. The word 'faith' can apply to every domain, to every circumstance in life. In order to understand this correctly, however, you should begin by replacing the word 'faith' by the word 'appreciation'. Yes, 'let it be done for you according to your appreciation', that is, according to the way you value and appreciate people and things.

People and things exist of themselves, events are what they are, but however beneficial they may

---

[6] Mt 8:13

be, neither people nor events can truly benefit or enrich us unless we contribute a factor of our own, and that factor is our consciousness, our thoughts and feelings, in other words, our respect and appreciation. It is our attitude which causes elements of another dimension and another power to be involved, elements which envelop the good things we receive with their spiritual emanations and thereby enhance their effectiveness.

To help you understand what I mean, let me begin by talking about Christian communion, the sacrament of the Eucharist. Communion is when the priest gives the faithful the host. As you know, the host represents the body of Christ, but what is it from the purely material, objective point of view? It is simply a mixture of wheat flour and a little water. The host is intended to serve as a reminder of the bread that Jesus gave to his disciples during their last meal together, when he said: *'Take, eat; this is my body.'*[7] But if it were enough to swallow a host in order to receive the body of Christ, any ordinary morsel of bread would do just as well, for it is almost the same.

Materially, a host gives you nothing more than you would get from a piece of bread – less perhaps – but of course it is not ordinary bread, it has a symbolic function: it represents Christ's body.

---

[7] Mt 26:27

Let it be done for you according to... 77

When a priest blesses a host he endows it with spiritual energies, and the faithful who receive it must allow themselves to be penetrated by its sacred meaning. For a host to become really and truly a host, it is not enough to make a little round wafer of wheat bread. The priest's blessing and the consciousness of those who receive the sacrament must be added to it. In the last analysis, therefore, it is the faithful who have the most important role to play, for it is they who, by their attitude, can negate what the priest's blessing has put into it. But it is also they who, by their faith, by their appreciation of what it represents, can reinforce that blessing.

The practice of Communion would be more effective if Christians understood the active role that is theirs. Yes, it is they who, by their attitude toward the host, have the possibility of enhancing the life-force God has given to the grain of wheat. God is life and he alone can give life. No one else has that power. When a grain of wheat has been transformed into a host, the role of the priest who blesses it is to bathe it in a spiritual fluid so that it may be given a more worthy reception by the soul and spirit of those who receive it.

Even if there were no priest to bless the host, a communicant who is conscious of the life that God has placed in it has the power to open a door within himself through which heavenly currents may enter. Contrary to the general belief, it is not the host that has this power. In itself the host has no power; it is human beings that endow it with power through their attitude. Knowing this you need not be surprised if I say that if you have an attitude of respect, gratitude and love toward your everyday food, you will also be performing a sacred act which will nourish not only your physical body but also your subtle bodies and even your soul and spirit.

We cannot receive more than that which we have prepared in our own mind. This is worth thinking about. It is how you consider things, your appreciation of things that counts and that produces results. You can see evidence of this in every area of life. For example, if you see your partner in life as an aspect, a manifestation of the Deity, you will be in touch through him or her with heavenly powers, and receive many blessings. But if you see your spouse as no more than a means of gratifying your sensuality you will be linking yourself to the brutish forces of the astral world and will have to endure the consequences.

It is because most people do not understand this truth that they get so little benefit from their relationships. If a woman ends by seeing only the negative aspects of her husband (his weakness, selfishness, crudeness, and violence) she will soon receive only unwholesome currents from him.

Let it be done for you according to...

Then, of course, she will feel that she is a victim, without realizing that she has contributed very largely to the situation. Every man is a representative of the heavenly Father, the cosmic spirit; every woman is a representative of the divine Mother, the universal soul. Yes, all the human beings around you, all men and all women, represent a divine principle, the masculine or the feminine principle. Whatever their shortcomings and imperfections, therefore, you must surround them with light and love, see them in the midst of light and love. In this way you will be giving them something, and through them you will receive light and love in return.

Human beings are extraordinary: they would all like to be able to influence people and things, but when they are given the means to do so either they pay no attention or they refuse them because they do not correspond to what they had hoped for or do not fit in with their point of view. But their point of view and what they hope for are good neither for others nor for themselves. What they want is to confront other people, to impose their own views and oblige them to do their will. Then if the others fail to comply they bombard them with bad thoughts and feelings and even physical ill-treatment. What a detestable way to behave!

If you want to influence others, begin by analyzing your attitude toward them. Even if they are as incompetent, stupid, selfish, dishonest, and evil as you think, you must stop focusing on their defects and broadcasting them to others, for in doing so you only reinforce them. Also, you do yourself harm by laying yourself open to their negative influence. This law is valid in every domain, and you must try to apply it in all your relations – with your family, friends, neighbours, colleagues at work, and also in the way you treat the objects around you.

From time immemorial human beings have had a natural tendency to attribute a special power to certain stones, to certain objects of wood or metal, even though they did not always have any particular form. By concentrating on them they transformed these objects into receptacles of cosmic forces. Stone menhirs or statues have always had – and continue to have – a role to play in all religions. By projecting all that is best in their hearts and souls onto statues which represent God or one of the saints, believers have transformed them into conductors for their prayers, and reciprocally, as conductors for the response of light, peace, and help from the invisible world. But is it only the sacred objects associated with religion that should be treated with consideration and respect? Do they have nothing in common with those that you use every day? You live in a house or apartment in which there are a number of

Let it be done for you according to...

different rooms, and in these rooms are all kinds of objects. If you have put them there it is because they are useful to you; you relate to them every day. Why not think of consecrating these objects? If you dedicate them to goodness and light they will have a favorable influence on you and your family. Once these things are consecrated, you must use them with care and attention, for the way you use them will reflect on you.

Now I'm not saying that you should treat your kitchen utensils in the same way as statues or holy pictures. I am simply drawing your attention to the importance for your inner life of your attitude to things. By your attitude you can transform the ordinary things around you into instruments of magic that are linked to heaven. In this way the energy in them will do you good. How is it possible that you still have not understood this? Certain experiences in your private lives ought to have alerted you to this truth a long time ago. Let me give you another example...

A young man and girl are strolling through a park. They are happy to be walking under the great trees and among the flowers, with birds singing all around. At one point the girl picks a flower and gives it to the boy. When he gets home, he puts the flower between the pages of a book to keep it safe. Very soon, of course, the petals fade and become discolored, but what does that matter? Every time the young man sees it he feels as though his sweetheart were smiling at him and using it to tell him a thousand and one things. He wears it close to his heart; he kisses it, and it is like a talisman which opens the gates of heaven for him. His joy is an inspiration to him and he becomes a poet. Then, as time passes and his relations with the girl seem less idyllic, he barely notices the flower between the pages of his book. It no longer has a message for him. It is as though it had become empty and voiceless, and finally he throws it away. What has happened? The flower is still there, still the same. It is he who has changed. It was he who made a talisman out of that flower and it is he who deprives it of its power.

The things you receive from someone else are impregnated with that person's emanations. But when they become yours you can either enhance the life that is in them or you can let it die. It all depends on your faith and love. It is important that you understand this. An object or being exists of itself, but its true existence will become manifest to you only if you open yourself to it. Yes, before a person or thing can truly exist, there must be two: it and you, for you, through your consciousness, your sensitivity toward it, give it life and a fuller presence.

This means that there are other ways of considering what you call 'inanimate objects.'

Let it be done for you according to...

Perhaps you will say: 'But is that really important? Objects don't feel anything. The way we treat them will cause them neither joy nor suffering.' That is true, but it is you who will receive joy or suffering. Everything you do produces currents, either positive or negative, harmonious or discordant, and those currents affect not only you but others beyond you, all beings near or far in both the visible and the invisible worlds. You are responsible for your own actions, because nothing you do is without consequences of which you will be either the victim or the beneficiary.

You must no longer be negligent, no longer ignore these truths, otherwise you will continue to grope your way through life complaining that you cannot see any sense in what you do. Heaven has led you to a knowledge of this teaching, so try at least to get something good out of it to advance your evolution, otherwise it will all be a waste of time.

All human beings try to find a meaning in life – although it sometimes seems as though they did everything possible not to find it. How can they find it if what they care most about is the gratification of their crudest instincts? If they took a good look at themselves they would see that they are animated only by the desire for pleasure and the need to dominate and possess. If you truly want to find meaning, you have to be detached, to put a little distance between yourself and things, otherwise you will be firmly glued in place and there will be no question of meaning.

God has placed the meaning of life in our understanding, respect, and love for all that he has created. We are free, of course, to use the things we need, but only on the condition that we do so without contravening the laws of love and respect; on the condition that we sense the pervading presence of an intelligence, of entities with whom we can communicate. Apart from anything else, human beings would have more consideration for each other if they habitually had a better attitude toward everything around them.

There is an infinite number of degrees in life, and if you want to savor the subtlest degrees, you must look beyond the physical appearance of creatures and sense the currents which emanate from every one of them – from rocks to the sun, from flowers to the stars – the currents which weave the mysterious fabric of creation. Each element of creation has its own kind of language. They speak to each other and they also speak to us, and it is up to us to learn to share harmoniously in this universal language. In this way we will come to understand that the only thing we need to do is find ways of improving the quality of our participation, and when we succeed, we will no longer ask useless questions about the existence

Let it be done for you according to... 85

of God, for we will sense that we are participating in divine life. What more can we ask?

Everything is alive; everything vibrates, everything radiates. If you were clairvoyant you would see the rays emitted by the whole of creation. But even if you cannot see, you can at least sense them, and that is even more important, because for our inner spiritual life sensation is superior to sight. It is possible to see without feeling anything. In fact this is exactly what most human beings do: they see but they do not benefit very much from what they see, because they are, as it were, locked into the depths of their own being, all doors and windows barred, and nothing can reach them. If God himself paid them a visit, they would probably be content to look at him and criticize, for there are many things in him that would displease them. Thus, profound change cannot be accomplished by sight, you also have to feel.

Since nature is alive, you can speak to her. Rocks, plants, rivers, mountains, and stars do not know our languages, but that is unimportant. Whatever language we use, all the words we utter with conviction and love produce vibrations, colors, and waves which influence matter, and matter responds as though it understood. I am not so naive as to think that when I speak to the earth, water, air, or fire they understand the words I use.

No, but those words produce specific effects depending on the thoughts, the feelings, and the force I put into them. When I speak to water, I know that my words are simply vehicles of pure forces which will touch the water, and in touching it they will create a kind of opening through which it will answer me and reveal many things to me. Yes, because water contains the archives of the planet since its beginning. In the course of its many journeys between the heavens and the earth, it has recorded everything.

Now, if it is possible to influence nature and inert matter, how much more possible is it to influence human beings. It is this that is really worthwhile; nothing is more useful than to learn to have a good influence on others. Who can deny that some of the greatest afflictions, the greatest misfortunes human beings have to endure, are those they continually inflict on each other – and by the same token, on themselves? Yes, just think! Because someone has done something which does not suit you, you begin to think of him as an enemy, and from then on you give a negative interpretation to everything he does. In reality, he is not your enemy; he has no desire to wrong you; in fact he does not even know what you hold against him. It is you who, by looking upon him in that way, have made an enemy of him and at the same time have destroyed something in yourself.

Let it be done for you according to...

So it is you who are your own enemy; it is you who have taken up arms against yourself. And now tell me: is that intelligent?

Human beings have an instinctive tendency to see the world through the lens of their own desires and fears. The whole of their psychic life is formed by subjectivity and imagination. But like all instincts, this too must be educated. Since people and things become within us what we believe them to be, there is need for a lot of work. First, we must be vigilant in order to avoid becoming our own victims by transforming into evil something that is merely neutral or even good. But we must also make an effort to transform what is evil and harmful into something beneficial.

Since thought possesses powers, we must use those powers to control the negative states we slip into so naturally and which poison our everyday life. The least little irritation immediately sets off an inner mechanism. Any occasion becomes an opportunity to ruminate on thoughts and feelings of exasperation, anger, and hatred. We interpret what other people do in the light of our own desires and expectations – and beware to those who do not meet those expectations! Not only do we resent them, but we also attribute all kinds of hostile intentions to them. We never think that perhaps they were busy or had been called away, that they had cares of their own, or were perhaps ill. We never think that their behavior may have been fully justified by their circumstances. Why bother ourselves with such questions? We prefer to interpret it as a personal insult. When, oh when will human beings realize that it is not others who do them the most harm? It is they who are their own worst enemies, because they never stop listening to their hypersensitive lower nature which feeds on false ideas and beliefs.

In the past, publishers did not produce very many books about esotericism and the occult sciences. Today it is different, and I find this phenomenon disturbing, for such books are now widely available and very popular. Many of them talk about magic and explain that anyone can use the power of thought accompanied by various rites and spells to influence events and other people – either for good or, of course, for evil – with the result that many of their readers tend to blame black magic for the difficulties they meet with in everyday life. An accident, an illness, a difficulty at work, and they immediately imagine that someone envies or resents them and is using black magic against them.

A few days ago I received a letter from a man who asked me to help him, because he was certain that the problems he was encountering were caused by black magic. To prove it, he gave me details, a multitude of details: the look a certain individual

Let it be done for you according to... 89

gave him, his words and gestures, and all the unfortunate coincidences that could only have been caused by the malevolent forces that person was sending his way. The list of his 'proofs' covered several pages... But do you want to know what I see when someone tells me tales like this? You will perhaps be surprised, but what I see above all is that if it is true that a black magician is involved, he will find his task greatly facilitated. Why? Because it takes only a look, a few words or gestures, and a few quite insignificant coincidences to trigger people's imagination... and it is they who do the rest. Yes, they interpret things and launch into extravagant flights of the imagination, so that it is they, in fact, who persecute themselves by failing to find the right attitude within themselves. As for 'black magicians', they need do hardly anything.

So I beg you, if you suffer a setback, an illness, an accident, or an estrangement, try first of all to look for the cause within yourself, and see what you should do to set things right. Don't waste valuable time in wild fantasies that will get you nowhere and only make your problems worse. I do not deny that black magic exists. Unfortunately, it does exist. I know that. But I also know something more important: it is our own attitude, our appreciation of things that gives us the power to amplify or minimize them. Since black magic exists, let us suppose that some ill-intentioned people want to use it against you: well, if you are strongly convinced of its power, you will amplify that power, but if you remind yourself that, as a son or daughter of God, you cannot be so easily affected by the forces of evil, you will remain unharmed. This is true faith. All the rest is no more than belief.

Let it be done for you according to your faith. Jesus said this in response to sick people who asked to be healed, but that does not mean that it cannot be applied in a broader context. If you wait to be ill before expressing your faith and asking for a miracle, you run the risk of being disappointed, and Jesus' words will not have been much help to you. So translate 'Let it be done for you according to your faith' as: 'people, objects, and events will be for you what your appreciation makes them'. In this way Jesus' words will help you in every situation in life. Thus, whatever the circumstance, remember to analyze yourself so that you know exactly what you are doing, and above all how you are doing it.

Suppose, for example, that your duties include certain tasks which are not particularly pleasant or interesting, and you have to do them every day. Whether they please you or not, whether they interest you or not, you cannot avoid them. Now, observe the way you behave when you have to do

Let it be done for you according to...

something you do not enjoy: you sigh and grumble and set about it without conviction or love. You do not realize that by your attitude you make your task even more unpleasant than it need be, and the efforts you are obliged to make will not only do you no good, but they will be actually destructive. On the other hand, if you learn to see things differently, if you make up your mind to use the tasks that bore you as an exercise and an opportunity to make progress, everything will be different.

I repeat: observe yourselves carefully, for our reactions to boring or unpleasant tasks are almost always instinctive – so deeply instinctive that we are not even conscious of them, and it is precisely then that we allow darkness and dissonance to enter us, and by letting them in we are weakening ourselves. This tendency to react negatively is linked to the idea we have of sacrifice. We fear and dislike sacrifice, because we think it means the loss of something. And because the sacrifices we have to make are usually for the sake of someone else, we think that it is they who gain whereas we lose. No, it is just the opposite, and if we understand it in the wrong way we will be cutting ourselves off from the source of life and joy.

If you say, 'Oh, I still have to do that, what a bore!' you will only succeed in putting insurmountable obstacles in your own path. But if you accept it willingly and with love, all obstacles will fall away and an ocean of light will break upon you and carry you away on its waves. Change your attitude and you will find that every gesture, every action, everything you have to do has the power to strengthen, cheer, and vivify you. Yes, your attitude... You can replace the word 'faith' by 'appreciation' but also by 'attitude'. The notion of attitude includes not only faith but also feeling and thought. Faith by itself is only a part, a limited manifestation of the human soul, and this is why it is inadequate if it is not backed up by other virtues.

Nothing is more important than to find the right attitude toward objects and creatures, above all toward our Creator. It is thanks to this attitude that you will take possession of your celestial heritage. And what is that heritage? Words are powerless to describe it; it is you who will discover it one day. In the meantime, work, learn, and train yourselves.

Our teaching is a school which prepares you to become heirs to heaven and earth, but to win your heritage, you have to turn to the Creator, your heavenly Father. And to turn to your heavenly Father implies that you close your doors to the entities and forces of darkness. Those who are open to all comers in the belief that it is possible to be open to God and at the same to the Prince of this world are in danger of losing everything.

Let it be done for you according to...

Unfortunately, many people – even Christians – are very adaptable. They say: 'I'm perfectly willing to serve God, but you never know... Will he listen to me and answer my prayers? Perhaps it would be better not to sever my links with the one who gives us all material riches, pleasure, money, and glory.' Many people – even without being fully aware of it – reason in this way. They have forgotten that Jesus said: *'No one can serve two masters; for a slave will either hate the one and love the other, or be devoted to the one and despise the other. You cannot serve God and wealth.'* [8]

The one thing that is essential is to find the right attitude toward all that exists, above all toward the Prime Cause, the Creator. If you have the right attitude toward the Creator, then wherever you may be all creatures – yes, the whole of creation from the angels to birds, trees, and mountains – will look on you with a smile. New currents and new joys will come to you, and you will go forward in the sure knowledge that life has meaning.

Heavenly entities will never bow before your powers, your wealth, your knowledge, or your prestige; they will bow only before your attitude, because it is your attitude that reveals whether or not you have understood what is essential. Make

---

[8] Mt 6:24

a very clear mental note of this and you will find that it is true; you will have plenty of time in which to confirm it. For my own part, I have already confirmed the truth of it, and now it is your turn to do so.

It is your attitude that will determine the kind of future you have. Once you understand this you can forget all the rest, because all the rest is contained in what I have just been telling you. Thus, *Let it be done for you according to your faith*, also means 'let it be done for you according to your attitude'. Our attitude is the face we turn to persons and things, an open, receptive face or one that is closed and hostile toward them. If you turn your face to heaven you will receive light and strength, but if you turn your back on heaven you will lose everything. The law is uncompromising; you cannot trifle with these things. If the scriptures tell us that God is just, it is because their authors knew this law.

Attitude is a magical power. Nothing happens to us that we have not brought upon ourselves by our attitude. It is our attitude that has the power to trigger this or that force in the universe. Thus we should turn to the divine world several times a day and bring ourselves into harmony with it until we are so perfectly adjusted to that world that our spiritual centers are suddenly set in motion, and waves, sounds, and colors flow out from us. Then

Let it be done for you according to...

our thoughts, feelings, and actions will reflect exactly and be as precious and as beautiful as that which exists on high in the heavens. The luminous entities which inhabit the heavens will recognize their own likeness in those who understand the purpose of their life on earth.

Chapter Six

ONLY OUR ACTIONS WITNESS TO OUR FAITH

The question of faith is so complicated that you cannot even rely on what people say when they declare themselves to be believers or unbelievers. Some claim to have faith, but when you see how they behave you cannot help but be astonished: at the least little thing they are worried, irritated, or discouraged; their behavior is egotistical, self-seeking, spiteful, and vindictive. Others, who say they are unbelievers, express thoughts and feelings of great nobility, and behave with self-mastery, kindness, tolerance, and selflessness. We have to ask ourselves finally what it means to have faith.

The truth is that the former cling to their religious beliefs, but do not have true faith, whereas the latter may have no set beliefs, but the divine law is written in their hearts, and it is this law that inspires all their actions.

In reality, the divine law is written in the hearts of all human beings. The only difference is that some, having worked on themselves, have succeeded in banishing the darkness from their psychic life and can read that law in their hearts every day, whereas others, who are still the slaves of their instincts, continue to obey the laws of their lower nature. But what is the use of believing in God if your faith does not transform you? A man says, 'I believe in God,' but there is nothing to show that his faith has done him any good. How can God's presence in a person be so feeble, so unproductive, and ineffective? If it has no better effect than that, is it worth believing in him?

The reaction of atheists is very understandable: when they see the meager benefits of faith in so many Christians, they conclude that they can get along perfectly well without God. Indeed, what is the use of proclaiming a God of justice and love and of praying for the coming of his kingdom on earth if at the same time we consider it normal to live lives of selfishness, hatred, and conflict?

Thus there are people who have no faith but who behave well, and others who have faith and behave badly, and this is a pity, as much for the former as for the latter. Why? Because those who behave naturally in accordance with the laws of justice, honesty, and kindness without consciously basing their actions on a spiritual principle, are deprived of something essential which could strengthen their convictions and give them courage in times of trial and adversity. How can human

Only our actions witness to our faith

beings imagine that the source of their most precious qualities is in themselves? How is it possible not to sense the existence of a higher Being, one who not only possesses the fullness of those qualities but who is their source?

But worse still is the situation of those who claim to believe in God and who do nothing – or almost nothing – to manifest the divine virtues. True faith admits of no separation, no divergence between what you believe and the way you live. Each man, each woman is a unit and must allow no contradiction in their lives. Of course, we cannot demand that everyone be perfect, but no one can be excused for not working toward perfection so as to give life to the divine model in whose image we are made.

Some might say: 'Oh, but priests and ministers have always told us that the important thing in God's eyes was to have faith.' I know, and in this they follow the teaching of St Paul whose epistles continually insisted on the need for faith. In his Epistle to the Romans, for instance, he wrote: *For we hold that a person is justified by faith apart from works prescribed by the law.* [9]

In reality we are saved neither by faith alone nor by good works alone, for they cannot be separated. It is useless to have faith if you do not

---

[9] Rm 3:28

act in accordance with that faith. And how can you act if you have no creed, no ideal? The two are linked. If, for centuries, the Church used St Paul to justify its insistence on the necessity of faith it was because it was in its own interest: it served to maintain its power. Yes, those who seek to dominate others – on whatever level: religious, political, or philosophical – know that the best way is not by exerting physical constraints but by influencing their minds, by imposing ideas and beliefs.

As a first step, it is true, we are right to emphasize the importance of faith, for the one thing human beings need most is to believe in a creative Principle, a Power that is infinitely greater than they – no matter what name they give it. By asking them to believe you are giving them an orientation, an invitation to raise their sights to a higher world. Even if they cannot immediately bring their actions into harmony with their faith in God, the awareness of the existence of a supreme Being will gradually become stronger and will incite them to strive to raise themselves to his level.

A few days ago I was strolling through the forest when I saw a tiny caterpillar climbing up the thread of a spider's web. The thread was so fine you could not even see it. The caterpillar twisted and turned, folding and unfolding itself, and its whole body participated in the effort as it climbed

Only our actions witness to our faith

with inexhaustible energy. When it finally reached the leaf at the top it settled down and began to eat. It had succeeded. It had not been afraid that the thread would break. Why am I telling you about this little caterpillar and its climb up the spider's thread? Because I want you to understand that heaven sends us invisible threads too.

Faith consists in taking hold of the threads sent by heaven and making the necessary effort to climb upward, without fear that they will break. Yes, like the caterpillar, we have to work hard to get to the top. If we have not understood this it is because we do not have faith, only beliefs. And as I have already explained: faith is one thing but beliefs are another. If you think you can be saved without exerting yourself that is only a belief. Too many Christians are content to accept the idea that they only need to believe to be saved. But to believe what? That Jesus has saved them by the sacrifice of his life on the cross? What an aberration! If you work, if you prepare yourselves, yes, then the power of Jesus will work through your own goodwill and will save you. Otherwise you need not expect anything. You will not be saved if you do nothing. Is this quite clear now?

Faith works, whereas belief waits. Belief declares: 'It is written that Christ will come on the clouds, that the angel will sound the trumpet, and then we shall all rise from the dead.' Yes... well you may wait a long time for that angel with the trumpet. He has already come and many have already risen from the dead, because they had true faith. They had worked actively; they had not been content to wait passively. So for us too, there is only one thing to do: to work, to prepare ourselves actively. It is useless to keep saying that we believe in God if we never bring ourselves to make an effort.

Faith gives us the key to fulfillment by creating the right conditions for the manifestation of the spirit. It is necessary for the groundwork, but it can produce beneficial results only if we find within ourselves the most fitting ways of manifesting it. Those who believe while continuing to behave in ways contrary to the laws of faith – the laws of the causal plane – destroy their own power. By their faith they build up; by their actions they tear down. They may imagine that their faith will save them. No, that would be too easy. People can believe in God – it is very comfortable, very reassuring to do so – and continue to behave like unbelievers. A great many criminals say that they have faith, but the question is: what kind of faith? One thing is certain: faith will not help them unless they decide to behave differently.

A faith that is not expressed in appropriate attitudes and behavior is almost useless, worse than useless in fact, because it allows people to go on deluding themselves. Faith can have no meaning

Only our actions witness to our faith

in your life unless it is accompanied by the will to act in accordance with it. Let us go back to the example of medicines: a doctor prescribes a medicine for you, and because it is prescribed by a doctor, you have faith in its efficacy. But if you are negligent and forget to take it you will continue to be ill. Whereas if you take it, it will be twice, three times, ten times more effective because of your faith in it. Faith does not do everything. You could say that it opens doors and windows, it makes certain things possible, it clears the way ahead for you. But if you have neither the will nor the strength to walk forward you will simply remain in front of the open road. Faith has opened the way, but what can happen if you do not move?

You might say: 'Are we to believe then that priests and ministers have misled us deliberately by their insistence on faith?' I do not know if that was what some intended... certainly not all of them. But one thing is sure, and that is that most of them are incapable of explaining faith clearly, and their notion of God is infantile, even ridiculous. According to them God wants human beings to believe in him and to demonstrate their belief by participating in all kinds of ceremonies in which they pray and sing his praises. If they do this he will be satisfied, and as the kind and merciful father he is, will forgive all their evil deeds. But tell me: do you know many parents who would accept such a situation? How many mothers or fathers would let their children behave as badly as they pleased as long as they proclaimed them as the greatest, the strongest, the wisest of parents – and not only allow bad behavior, but dedicate themselves to saving the children from the consequences of their wrongdoing? No father with a grain of common sense would agree to such a thing. And yet we are asked to believe that this is what God accepts and appreciates.

Of course God is kind and merciful, but what does that mean? It means that he does not expect us *always* to dominate ourselves. What he expects of us is that we have a clear idea of the direction we should take, that we make an effort to keep to the right path, and that we repair our errors along the way. If we do fall from time to time, we must not lose courage and lie where we fell: we must pick ourselves up and go on. God cannot accept that human beings use faith to minimize or excuse their faults.

The Church's insistence on faith has only served to lead believers into error. It is so reassuring to tell yourself: 'Since it is faith that saves, it does not matter too much if I do something wrong. Life is hard and I have to get along as best I can. Even if I am not always honest, kind, or generous my faith will save me.' Well, no! Divine laws exist, and those laws will not be swayed by

Only our actions witness to our faith

the faith of those who behave badly, whatever reasons they find to justify themselves.

Faith is necessary, indispensable, that goes without saying. But whether you believe or not, it is what you do that counts. For centuries, those who doubted, for example, that Jesus was the only son of God, were considered to be the worst kind of criminals. Even if they manifested all the Christian virtues of kindness, justice, love, and self-sacrifice, they were liable to be burned at the stake. Whereas those who destroyed whole cities and massacred so-called heretics and infidels in the name of Jesus, were seen as ardent defenders of the faith and were praised by all. To contravene the laws of justice and love taught by Jesus was of no great consequence, but to doubt a dogma proclaimed by the Church, that was a crime.

Those who treat others with goodwill, understanding, patience, and generosity are – whether they know it or not – manifesting faith in a higher principle which dictates their conduct. As for those who imagine that their faith will erase their faults in the eyes of God, they are doubly mistaken. In the first place it is not true that it will erase them, and in the second place they are behaving dishonestly – which only makes their case worse – for it is a mockery of God to claim to believe in him while doing the opposite of what he asks. If faith is enough, why are so many believers floundering in deplorable situations where their faith can do nothing to help them? What is the good of their repeating, 'I believe; I believe!' if at the same time another voice in the depths of their being can be heard saying, 'I am weak; I am ill; I am ignorant.'? It is time to forget all these false ideas about faith. The only thing that really counts is what we do.

This is why I say – and may I be forgiven for saying it – that when Christians ask God to look only at their faith and not at their sins they are behaving childishly. In the first place God does not look at our sins. He has many other better and more beautiful things to look at. He is not like human beings who take pleasure in observing and commenting on other people's faults and failings. Why do we attribute to God our own unwholesome taste for manifestations of stupidity and ugliness? Some of you may say: 'But if God punishes us for our faults, it is because he sees them.' No, when we commit a fault it is not God who punishes us. It is we ourselves, for our faults create disorder in our minds, our hearts, and our souls, and the negative repercussions of that disorder can be felt in the whole of our existence. That is what our 'punishment' is: a consequence that we ourselves have set in motion.

God does not turn away from human beings, neither does he punish them. It is they who, by

Only our actions witness to our faith

their faults, turn away from him, and when they do this they inevitably experience coldness, darkness, and every kind of restriction. They reason as though their actions were purely exterior to themselves and could in some way be detached from them. Well, no: all our acts, whether good or evil – even when they are exterior to ourselves – leave traces within us, and these traces cannot be erased. This being so, how can we ask God to look only at our faith and not at our acts? There is only one way to resolve the problem: straighten out the situation, that is, bring our actions into line with our faith.

Whatever your words may say, only your attitude can prove that you have faith. Through your attitude it can be seen that your faith is sustained by your love, your intelligence, your knowledge, and your will. To believe in God is to feel that you are the son or daughter of God and consequently to act in accordance with that kinship. The sons and daughters of God know not only that they are heirs to the virtues and powers of their heavenly Father and Mother, but that they must do everything possible to cultivate those virtues and powers and thus become masters of their own destiny. Every act that is not inspired by genuine wisdom and love produces a dark miasma within you and becomes an obstacle to the manifestation of the Deity. How can people speak of faith if they do nothing to cleanse and purify the space between themselves and God?

Wrongdoers invite entities of darkness to enter them, and however vociferously they declare that they believe, once they have got themselves into this deplorable situation nothing can save them. I repeat: faith can only prepare the ground so that we may do what is right. If we want to irrigate the ground, we dig trenches. If we want to light our house, we install electric wiring. And if we want to receive radio or television programs, we buy equipment with the circuits to receive and transmit sound and pictures. I could give you a multitude of examples to show that it is by their actions that human beings can dig the trenches and install the electrical circuits within themselves that will receive and transmit divine energies. How can we imagine that God's love, wisdom, and will can find a pathway within us if we have not planned or prepared anything? That path will be built by your actions, but also by the thoughts and feelings which inspire them. If there is no pathway prepared for them, the divine energies which flow through space will not enter you, they will flow elsewhere.

When you invite someone to stay with you, you do not just invite him without thinking of where he will sleep: you prepare a room for him. And how much more so if your guest is someone important. Before sending your invitation you think

Only our actions witness to our faith

about how you are going to welcome him. Imagine, for instance, that you are expecting a prince to stay: are you going to receive him wearing slippers and an old bathrobe? Are you going to welcome him into a dirty, untidy house? Well, may I be forgiven again by Christians if I say they want to treat God in ways that they would not dare to inflict on their neighbor. They invite him into a pigsty. And then they are astonished when it is not God but demons who respond to their invitation.

So many people complain that they have faith and pray every day but that God does not hear their prayer. 'My life is full of difficulties, I'm always unhappy, always ill. My life has no more meaning.' Well, whose fault is that? If you are always battling against difficulties it is because you have brought them on yourself. 'But that is not what I asked for. I didn't know...' Yes, well whether you knew or not, you have broken certain laws and now you are suffering the consequences. If you fail to respect the highway code the police will fine you. It will be no good saying: 'But sir, I didn't know that...' He will just go on writing out your ticket. He does not want to hear about whether you knew the law or not. As far as he is concerned you should know. So from now on try to match your behavior with your faith. For if you break the rules now that you can no longer plead ignorance, you will be doubly guilty and will suffer in consequence.

Human beings are really peculiar: they think it is enough for them to kneel down in a church or temple and recite a few prayers to feel themselves in the presence of God. No, you cannot sense the presence of God unless you wash away some of the dirt from within. Just as the light of the sun cannot shine through a window covered in dust or soot, so the divine presence cannot penetrate those who have not cleared away their inner impurities. There is always work to be done in this respect. This is why, every morning and every evening, you must think about this necessary purification. By analyzing your inner attitudes, thoughts, and feelings, and by endeavoring to guide them in the direction of good, you will become like a transparent crystal through which the light of heaven can shine. Only then will your faith be revealed by your acts.

As you see, I give you all these examples to show you that, in nature as in our own lives, everything can serve to instruct us. Of course, if you prefer to cling to your illusions and run the risk of bringing disaster on yourself and others, you are free to do so. What can I do about it? You are free to accept or refuse. For my part, I am free only to explain.

Many people imagine that a spiritual Master has the power to oblige human beings to change. Not at all! However great the love, wisdom, and

Only our actions witness to our faith

power of a Master, people who are dull-witted and have closed minds will not be touched by them. It is always possible to find ways of imposing your will on the physical plane, but not on the psychic plane. And a Master has no desire to coerce human beings. A genuine spiritual Master knows the laws, and he knows that he has no power over those who are immured in their own beliefs. Of course, he talks, he tries to convince, he presents his arguments because his dearest wish is to help people, but he knows very well that only those who are prepared and open will accept the light he has to offer. He leaves the others alone. But life does not leave people alone. Life is implacable. Every now and then, those who do not want to know and respect the divine laws receive a few buffets from life.

Chapter Seven

NEVER ABANDON YOUR FAITH IN GOOD

One day a man told me of the problems he was having with a friend. Because of a misunderstanding between them their relations had become difficult, and the hostile attitude of his one-time friend hurt him deeply. My visitor explained: 'I really wish we could make up. I pray for that every day and ask God to help me. I concentrate and work mentally, but there seems to be no improvement.' After listening to him for a moment, I said: 'All that activity is magnificent. But why call on all the heavenly powers to help in such a tiny problem which you could perfectly well settle for yourself? A friendly look, a few words, a generous gesture... that is all it would take for this person to understand that you are still his friend. You want to get God to intervene – a very difficult undertaking – to solve your problems. Try instead to use the very simple means he has given you: a look, a word, a gesture.'

So many believers do not really know what faith is or how it can help them. Well, among other things, faith is the certain knowledge that the Creator has not left his creatures destitute, helpless and unarmed, that he has given them all the necessary means to provide for their material, emotional, and intellectual needs. Instead of taking responsibility for themselves and learning to put all those means to work at the service of good, these unfortunate 'believers' kneel down to concentrate, pray, and implore heaven. And then, as nothing happens, they end by doubting the power of thought and prayer, sometimes even by doubting the existence of God. Since he has not answered their prayers, since he has failed to protect them, since he always allows the wicked to get the upper hand, they are not going to believe in him any longer. Do they really imagine that their reaction matters to God?

God has nothing to gain from the faith of human beings, and nothing to lose from their lack of faith. He is so rich in himself. Heaven and earth are his; even we are his. Whether we believe in him or not we still belong to him, and since we belong to him he could well put us up for sale. He could not charge very much, of course, because there would not be many customers...

No need to be scandalized... let me have my little joke!

Never abandon your faith in good

We need to reflect on all this. Those who have learned to observe themselves and analyze their inner attitudes understand that to try and settle scores with God gets them nowhere, for it is they who lose something very precious. They begin to sense that their attitude creates a void within them, that they are depriving themselves of the presence of God, of his light, his beauty, his goodness, his strength, and his life. Yes, above all, his life. The only solution is to turn back to God, to tell him: 'O God, how stupid I've been! I thought I could get along without you and now I'm more miserable than ever.' Until people understand this, they can only add spiritual distress to their moral and physical distress. By cutting themselves off from the source of life, light, and love, they deprive themselves of all that sustains, nourishes, and inspires them, for that source is within them. By denying the existence of God they are denying the source of living water which nourishes their own existence.

Whatever your misfortunes, therefore, instead of making them a reason to abandon your faith in good, use them to strengthen your bond with the Godhead so that your spirit can regain control of the situation. In this way you will feel that you are freeing yourself, for the spirit is free. It is above events. When you restore the spirit to its rightful place within you, something tells you that it is not these little obstacles and irritants that have the power to make you lose your convictions, your peace, or your love. On the contrary. All the luminous experiences you have already enjoyed have taught you which values you can rely on, and it is those experiences you must cling to. Never doubt the great and beautiful things you have known; keep them with you as provisions for the difficult path that still lies ahead. And once the torment is past, you will see that what might once have caused you to lose your faith has in fact strengthened it.

The one thing that is most often mentioned by non-believers as a reason to doubt the existence of God is the fact of evil. 'If God existed,' they say: 'He would not allow so many crimes to be committed. All the evil that human beings do to their fellows... If God existed...' So it is because of their consideration for others, because they profess to love their neighbor that they deny the existence of God. All right, but tell me this: in the ordinary way, do many people really care about the good of their neighbor? Oh of course: they are affected briefly when they see pictures of devastation, famine, or other disasters on television. They may even shed a few tears. But they soon forget. The next minute they go back to the causes of their habitual discontent: the boss who exploits them, a competitor who has

Never abandon your faith in good

supplanted them, a neighbor who has encroached on their land, their husband, wife, children, or mother in law... The world's miseries are the least of their worries.

I am not saying that you should neglect personal problems. I am simply saying that people are more concerned with the petty difficulties they meet with in daily life than with the major disasters that affect others. Doesn't everybody know this? Yes, of course they know it, but they continue as before. In the face of the misfortunes that afflict humankind people declare that the world is in a sorry state, and having said that they have said it all. The world is in a sorry state – but they, of course, are impeccable. But who do they take themselves for? Above all, what do they ever do to improve the state of the world? They talk and complain and get angry, and while they are busy talking, complaining, and getting angry, evil continues its work. And it is all God's fault, because he does nothing to stop it.

As I have often said, the devil – for the sake of convenience, let's say the devil – has one quality. Only one, but it is an extraordinarily important one: he is active, energetic, tireless. Whereas good people are always feeble and easily fatigued. They are content to be amiable and inoffensive. When they have done a few good deeds they are pleased with themselves and think it is time to have a rest.

Who knows when they will get back to work? Good does not stimulate them in the way that evil stimulates the wicked, but whose fault is that? It is certainly not God who prevents them from improving themselves, who prevents them from adopting a brotherly attitude and working for the good of society.

The question is: do human beings really want good to prevail? We might well wonder. If they really wanted it they would manage to bring it about. So many tragedies are caused by people who, while saying that they only want to do what is right, are incapable of a reasonable reaction to a minor inconvenience or a trivial injustice. They want what is right, yet on the slightest pretext they precipitate interminable conflicts. So many wars have their origin in some trifling incident which no one attempted to control at the beginning and which was allowed to degenerate. Everyone knows this, but does anyone draw a lesson from it for the future? Do people often say to themselves: 'Let's see, what would be the best way to react to this or that difficulty? If I take such and such an attitude, if I take this or that decision, shall I be helping to improve matters or making them worse?' No? Then why accuse God when a situation gets out of hand? Is it he who whispers in people's ears the words we hear so often: 'One man's joy is another man's sorrow'?

Never abandon your faith in good

People say that they pity those who suffer, and yet they always manage to profit from their misfortunes. A business goes bankrupt? 'Excellent: we'll get their customers.' Two countries go to war? 'Great: we'll sell arms to both sides.' And so on and so forth. You only have to look around you: people's lives – their personal lives as well as that of the collectivity – are full of calculations of this kind. Is that God's fault? If a great many people genuinely cared about the well-being of their fellow human beings they could improve things tremendously. But they are content to observe and deplore the situation: 'How is it possible? Why do such things happen? How horrible!' Their disapproval does not prevent them from benefiting from other people's misfortunes if they can. No wonder the devil's business is still thriving!

More serious than all this is the fact that although human beings deplore evil and wish for good, it seems that they are far more convinced of the power of evil than that of good. Experience shows, they say, that those who wish to destroy people and disrupt society succeed more easily and more quickly than those who wish to make themselves useful and improve the situation, and since this is so, what is the use of all their efforts? They become discouraged, stop trying to react, and even let themselves be led into evil ways. But in considering the apparent victories of evil, there is one question they have forgotten to ask: how long will this victory last? Yes, in order to draw a really valid conclusion you have to consider the time factor, the question of duration. You will always miscalculate the situation if you forget that whenever evil goes into action the forces of good also rise up to combat it.

Cosmic intelligence has not given equal power to good and to evil. But how can we convince human beings of this when most of them claim to see only the triumph of evil wherever they turn? The fact is that their observations do not take in the whole picture. They see someone who behaves dishonestly, spitefully, and with violence. They see that he begins by succeeding: he imposes his will on others; he manifests his independence; he achieves his ambitions. Yes, but what will become of him in the future? He is going to find more and more obstacles in his path; his life will be full of complications; he will lose his peace of mind, and his health will give way. Then we see someone else who dedicates himself to the service of good: to begin with he will encounter great difficulties, but in spite of those difficulties he will have the support of the powers of light. As time goes on, he will encounter fewer obstacles, and those around him will begin to understand and appreciate him and give him their support.

Never abandon your faith in good

The good exists. Not only does it exist, but with the passage of time we are forced to realize that it always ends by being victorious. Never give way to discouragement, therefore, on the pretext that you see the ravages of evil in the world. Evil wins some battles and you feel threatened by it, that is normal, but that is no reason to lose your faith in good. If your faith in good is not steadfast, it means that you do not even have faith in the good that is in yourself. Suppose that nothing but evil surrounded you – which is certainly not the case – you could still cling to the good that is in you; you could still strengthen and intensify it. Is this certainty, this activity not something which could give meaning to your life, whatever your circumstances?

If there is one thing you must be absolutely sure of it is that good always ends by triumphing over evil, just as life always triumphs over death. The reality of death is only apparent. If you look around you, you will see only life. Life is everywhere. Death is nowhere. It is no more than a change of scene and of costume. You will perhaps say: 'But if someone murders a man, that's the end.' No, for in the first place only the physical body can be killed. The immortal spirit lives on, and after a while it comes back to earth in a new body. As for the murderer, he will be punished, and in one way or another will have to pay for his crime. He may manage to escape human justice but he will not escape divine justice.

At first sight, therefore, evil and death may seem to be victorious, but their victory does not last. Whereas, although good meets with opposition to begin with, it is good which prevails in the long run, just as life prevails over death. We only need to be patient. God has infinite patience; only human beings are impatient because they base their calculations on human measurements, on their own notion of time.

There may be some who will say: 'But I always want to do what is good. I pray for good to prevail. I ask God to guide me on the path of righteousness, and yet I often fail... I always seem to be doing something wrong. Why doesn't God stop me from straying?' Naturally, it is God's fault once again; they themselves are blameless. They want only to act for the best but God does not respond to their noble sentiments. If he can't even do that, what use is he? They really don't need him. Well, if these admirable beings truly desire only good they will have to manifest a little more honesty and sincerity. They desire good, but on the condition that it is easy to achieve and does not upset their personal plans, on the condition that it does not interfere with their need for comfort, pleasure, riches, power, or glory. In these conditions what can God possibly do?

Never abandon your faith in good

God leaves us free to do as we please, to go our own way. There are some who are determined to make mistakes and he lets them do so. He is patient. He knows they will eventually have to return to the right path. If their ideal of righteousness, kindness, and generosity were genuine they would receive an inner warning about the path to take, and even if they had set off in the wrong direction, they would be inspired to stop and turn back before going too far.

Many people seek goodness as others seek truth and never find it, because truth is a princess, a very demanding mistress, and what they are really seeking is a servant who will make life easier for them. Like truth, good is also a demanding mistress. If you claim to seek only good and yet you find evil, the fault is not God's but yours. If he lets you go astray, it is because you need to realize that you do not have a high ideal. When the choices you make lead to disappointment, conflict, or failure, ask yourself why your sense of direction is so faulty. We all have a kind of inner magnet which is the synthesis of our thoughts, feelings, and desires, and this magnet attracts the people and situations that correspond to the elements of our psychic life.

So as soon as you feel you may have taken the wrong turning, begin by restoring order to your inner world so that you will be more clear-sighted when choosing your way in the future. Of course it is difficult. Of course you will suffer. But that suffering – which you call evil –actually represents the warning signs which cosmic intelligence sends to all of us. It is a rude awakening from sleep and an invitation to reflect and understand that we need to change direction and exert ourselves. It is this so-called evil which enables us to avoid the final catastrophe that would wipe us off the face of the earth. So it is actually a divine good: it is a call to order by cosmic intelligence.

Never forget that behind all our difficulties and suffering there is a wisdom that is watching over us, and it is up to us to discover and decipher the goals and the laws of this wisdom. The understanding gained in this way enables us to see the link between our suffering and that wisdom, and from this encounter a light is born which shows us how God's power works within us, how it transforms our sorrows into joy, our weaknesses into strength, our darkness into light. Instead of letting our misfortunes become a pretext for losing our faith in good we should, on the contrary, use suffering as an opportunity to allow his power to penetrate us ever more profoundly.

All human beings who incarnate on earth, however highly evolved they may be, bear within them the seeds of the two worlds, the higher and the lower. A baby in a cradle is all innocence, but

Never abandon your faith in good

wait and see what he will become a few years later... It is a characteristic of a human being to be both divine and animal. Yes, it is the co-existence of these two natures, animal and divine, which make us human. We cannot separate the two; we have to let them grow together and work to adjust them to each other. It is this adjustment that makes it possible to pursue our life on earth. If you ask a great Master why evil exists he will not answer you, he will simply teach you to look on it as a raw material which you have to mold and shape in order that it may collaborate in the manifestation of good.

Faith in good is one of the essential foundations of our psychic life. If we do not have this faith we are in danger of losing whatever qualities and faculties we possess. Why? Because the foundations that guarantee the stability of those qualities are absent, and at the first opportunity, negative elements such as fear would prevent us from manifesting them. This is not difficult to understand: those who no longer believe in good believe in evil, and this automatically reflects in the way they reason, in their attitudes. Their lives are dominated by fear, for people and circumstances all seem suspect to them. And when they are in the grip of fear many people are guilty of cowardice, injustice, even cruelty. Despite all their good qualities they allow themselves to be overwhelmed by this irrational, uncontrollable instinct. Afterwards, when their fear has abated, they are often ashamed of what they did, but once it is done... If you want to defeat fear, you must have unshakable faith in the power of good, that is, in the supremacy of the spirit in a human being.

One day Master Peter Deunov said: 'The world needs teachers for evil and believers for good.' We need to believe in good and to learn to use evil, but we cannot learn to use evil unless we believe in good. Oh I know: it is difficult. As soon as evil manifests we suffer, and then not only do we find it difficult to believe in good but we even begin to doubt the existence of God. When your life is effortless and pleasant it is easy to imagine that you have faith. Oh yes, you believe that you believe... But *what* do you believe? That is another matter...

People's degree of evolution can be measured by their capacity to preserve their faith in good. It is this that teaches us to endure trials, to work on them and receive blessings from them. Then those trials become like deep valleys in the midst of mountains: waters from the peak flow into them, transforming them into fertile dales, and the best kinds of fruit trees flourish in their soil. Whereas those whose faith in good is destroyed by suffering are like barren rocks on which nothing but a little moss or lichen can grow. Suffering obliges human

Never abandon your faith in good

beings to descend into the depths of their being. As all other avenues are closed, they are obliged to call on the powers of their soul and spirit, and when they succeed in doing so, instead of moaning and groaning or crying out in revolt, they emanate a delicious perfume.

True faith is the ability to remain steadfast in the midst of tribulations, because tribulations are superficial accidents which do not affect our essence. Look at the ocean: however great the disturbance on the surface, the waters below are calm and still with no sign of turmoil. But when I say we must remain steadfast, that does not mean that we should become insensitive and incapable of emotion. No, even though we may feel pulverized, wiped out, we can still be aware that our suffering has meaning, that one day it can be utilized for good. So when you suffer, don't ask God to take your suffering away. Since it has been given to you for a reason he will not take it away, he will wait until you have learned all there is to learn from it.

God is not there to respond to our need for peace, tranquility, and well-being. He is concerned only with what will make us grow. He wants to make us wise, good, and free like himself. For all the rest we have to get along by ourselves with the means he has given us. Yes, but human beings get everything mixed up. They pray... Well, prayer is excellent, it is a force, but you have to know when and how to use that force.

When you are suffering the only thing you should ask of God and the luminous beings that inhabit the universe is that they teach you to bear your suffering so that you may obtain all the benefits it contains. Suffering does not exist in order to hurt us but in order to teach us where true good lies and to make us stronger, more intelligent, and more alive. Yes, those who have learned how to suffer become more vital and more expressive: a refinement, a kindness, a nobility can be read in their features. So tell yourselves every day that suffering conceals a secret knowledge which you must acquire, and that you should be joyful even in the midst of trials. And when I tell you this, I want you to know that I tell myself the same thing, for all of us without exception have to perfect ourselves; we all have to pass exams.

As long as we do not know how thought works, how conviction works, how faith works, we are depriving ourselves of the best ways of advancing our evolution. In the present stage of development of the planet and of the human race it is impossible not to encounter evil and suffering, and this is why the earth is seen as a school, a training center for those who are willing to learn, but also a reformatory for the wayward. Yes, the earth is the arena of evolutionary progress, and in order to

Never abandon your faith in good

evolve we have to learn to work with all forms of evil and therefore to experience difficulties and suffering. When the entities of the invisible world see 'parcels' marked 'destination earth', they immediately know what that means. The poor wretches in those parcels are the only ones who do not know what is in store for them. The earth contains such beauty and wealth, and they imagine that life is going to be agreeable, that they will enjoy ease and comfort. Well, they are mistaken.

Instead of lamenting the situation and complaining that the world is a 'vale of tears', instead of trying to understand why God does not intervene and wipe out evil, it would be better to preserve our faith in good and start working to perfect ourselves. Otherwise what possible use will our lives be? Not only will we have suffered but we will have learned nothing, understood nothing. Those who accept their difficulties and trials release the powers of their soul and spirit, and after a while they see that they have produced something magnificent. This is true alchemy: to transform raw matter, darkness, and suffering into a precious substance that shimmers and gleams with a thousand iridescent colors. Those who do not know how to suffer are always very poor, and when they want to express themselves they do not have the material they need. They know nothing of the life of the soul and spirit, of its immensity, its depths, or its summits, and for this reason they cannot be creators.

True creators, all those who, in whatever domain, achieve something great, have experienced great suffering. It is as though their suffering were the black ink in which they dipped their pens in order to produce works of extraordinary intelligence and beauty. Their experiences, the suffering they endured, all those feelings, sensations, and emotions are the paints with which they produced a great work of art or a sublime action from which all benefited... from which we benefit even today.

Some of you may say: 'When I hear what you say about suffering I am beginning to love it, I almost feel that I want to suffer.' Well, you must not exaggerate! You need not worry about looking for suffering: it will look for you. No one who ever lived on earth has been exempt from all trials. So instead of racing off to make war on evil in your desire to win the palm of martyrdom, be content to learn to overcome the difficulties you meet with every day. You must not be like those who look forward to accomplishing acts of heroism, but who, in the meantime, cannot put up with the slightest inconvenience and make life unbearable for everyone else.

You must never choose to do something simply because it is difficult, in the mistaken notion that

Never abandon your faith in good

your actions will be admired by others and approved by heaven. There is a Bulgarian proverb that says an over-zealous saint is an abomination in the sight of God. Yes, that kind of zeal is suspect. There are people whose temperament urges them to sacrifice themselves for a noble cause. It is their ideal of generosity that drives them to undertake something difficult almost in spite of themselves, and it is their ideal that saves them from being discouraged or crushed by evil. But we have to admit that such beings are rare. Beware of fanatics who commit senseless acts for the glory of martyrdom! It is useless for them to expect to gain the blessing of heaven that way; the only thing they will accomplish is their own destruction.

Not everyone is destined for heroism, but everyone must try to accept and rise above the daily trials of life. This is the only way to avoid even greater suffering, which might then become insurmountable. If you have never practised you will always be weak and impotent. So instead of seeing evil as a proof of the inexistence of God, you must accept it and work with it. As soon as you accept it, a train of events is set in motion within you, machines hum and begin grinding up that raw material so that it may be transformed.

Try it – if only for the sake of curiosity – for one week. Tell yourself: 'I don't like this philosophy. It goes against my habits and my way of looking at things... but I'll give it a try.' Then as each occasion arises, instead of cursing and lamenting and pestering heaven and earth with your recriminations, work with your thoughts. The first phase of this work is to be vigilant, that is, to avoid being carried away by anger, discouragement, hatred, and so on, as soon as something happens to upset you. For once you let yourself go it becomes more difficult to reverse the reaction.

Whatever the circumstances, disciples of an initiatic school must never abandon their faith in good; they must ask God to help them to remain faithful to their task. Countless invisible entities are there to prepare the way for our success, our happiness, but we refuse to acknowledge it. Why? Because events never turn out exactly as we expect or imagine they should. But if what we hoped for came about it might bring even greater complications and disappointments. Have you thought of that?

Divine wisdom answers our requests, but it does so through events that we do not understand. Yes, because we do not have the clairvoyance that would enable us to interpret the signs that point to the reason for those events, for the encounters we have, or for the presence of certain people around us. Instead of complaining and rebelling or becoming discouraged, we need to reflect and question ourselves: why did heaven decide that in

Never abandon your faith in good

our family, our job, or here in the brotherhood, we should be accompanied by these particular individuals and not by others? We need to learn to look at these difficult conditions from a different angle, and even if we still cannot understand them, to make the effort to realize that they mean something, that they are there for a reason. And the more incomprehensible they are, the more unlike anything we hoped for, the more we need to trust the heavenly powers that send them and tell ourselves that our highest aspirations will be accomplished through them.

With all the methods this teaching gives you, through your inner work, and through prayer you are gradually learning to rise above circumstances. Even if you are suffering now, after a while you will find yourself growing stronger and more serene, your relations with others will improve and you will feel the beneficial results of your work even for your health.

Suffering is very unpleasant – no need to tell me that! – but why increase your suffering by adding anger, rebellion, and discouragement so that you end by losing faith in the essentials: divine wisdom and love? Since we have to suffer, since we cannot avoid trials and tribulations, it would surely be more intelligent to use them to become richer rather than poorer. I am not saying that when you suffer you should behave as though you felt nothing, as though pain did not exist. No, pain is a reality, a terrible reality. If you question certain people who have been persecuted and made to suffer atrociously, they will tell you that, at the time, their only desire was for someone to come and release them from the abyss into which they felt they had been pitched. But years later they recognized that their experiences had enriched and strengthened them. They did not regret having been obliged to endure them.

So when you suffer, remember that one day you will look on that experience as an enrichment, and the thought of that will be doubly useful. First, because it corresponds to the reality – painful though it is today, it will be beneficial in the long run – and it is always a good thing to bear this truth in mind. Second, because when you formulate this thought it helps you to be detached about what you are going through; it allows you to stand back from it, to rise above it, and thus to put up with it more easily. This is an example of the power of thought: it helps us to stand off from what we are enduring.

Even among spiritualists there are not many who are capable of this inner attitude. They will treat you to learned discourses about karma, quoting complicated Sanskrit terms and references from all the Indian books on the subject. They will tell you that the law of karma is the law of cause and effect, the law of justice, that certain acts lead

Never abandon your faith in good

to certain consequences in the future, and so on. But as soon as they themselves are affected by evil they rebel and complain, wondering why God did not protect them. All of a sudden they forget that the earth is a school and that they too have to attend that school. They may be more highly evolved than most human beings, but they still have much to learn.

Yes, if we are here on earth it is for a reason, otherwise the Lords of Destiny could have sent us to another region of the universe: to Jupiter or Sirius for example. There are certainly many regions of the universe in which souls could go for a pleasant holiday, just as Russians go to their dachas or the English used to go to the French Riviera. Oh yes, there must be places like that in the universe that have not yet been discovered by astronomers. What do we know about the universe?

Actually, the best place to go is the sun. 'The sun?' you will say; 'we would be burnt alive!' Of course, if you went there with your physical body you would be a little too hot, but who said you should go with your physical body? The place for the physical body is the earth, it is designed for life on earth, but we have other bodies for the other planets or the sun. There are different forms of life in the universe corresponding to different aspects of matter. In any case, at the moment we are on earth so we cannot go to the sun with our physical bodies, but we can at least go there with our soul and spirit, with our thoughts and our love.

Well, if you understand what I have being saying today, you will begin by taking a fresh look at what you call evil, at all the things that afflict you, give you pain, and make you unhappy. In the light of these explanations you will see things clearly for the first time, and whatever your circumstances you will never give up your faith in good.

Chapter Eight

'UNLESS YOU BECOME
LIKE CHILDREN'

Television is a very useful instrument for the observation of the state of society. Even though the programs are not all very instructive or interesting, it can teach us a good deal about the world in which we live. This is why, when I have a free moment, I often watch TV for a few minutes, just to see what is going on.

When I switched it on the other day I found myself in the middle of a program in which a young man of about twenty-five was declaring: 'I don't believe in God, I don't believe in Buddha, I don't believe in Jesus, I don't believe in the Gospels...' And that was not all. The list of all the things he did not believe in went on for a long time: politics, society, the family... But what he rejected most violently was all notion of God and religion. At the end he said: 'I believe only in myself,' and you could see that he was very pleased with himself for – as he thought – creating such an excellent impression.

Now tell me: what is the use of bringing a young man like this in front of the cameras to talk such nonsense? And since he had the privilege of expressing himself before millions of viewers, how many young people would be led to think that this was the height of wisdom, this was the way to go: to believe in nothing and nobody except yourself? The poor wretch! I watched his face, his gestures, and the way he held himself, and it was obvious to me that the 'self' he believed in so firmly would never be much help to him.

You have to believe in yourself, of course, but in your divine self. In fact, you must not only believe in it, but you must give it the conditions it needs to manifest. How could a young ignoramus discover his divine self and manifest it if he rejects everything, including God and all those who could help him by giving him a philosophy and the methods he needs for that inner work? Young people are more and more inclined to think that it is a proof of independence to say that they want nothing to do with religion. They think that if they believed in God they would be limiting themselves and forfeiting their freedom. Well, all right: they do not believe in God but they believe in pleasure, power, money, glory, the opinion of their friends... and they call that freedom. What can anyone do to help such poor simpletons? They think that they would be enslaved by God, that is, by light, love,

'Unless you become like children' 145

and kindness, and to free themselves they use the very means that will most effectively enslave them. They do not realize that they are closing the doors of heaven against themselves, and that one day, inevitably, the doors of the earth will also be closed to them.

Some people say: 'For my part, I refuse to bow either before God or before men, and no doors are closed to me. Wherever I go I am welcomed, respected, listened to...' Yes, but you are blind, my friend. You cannot see that the doors of heaven are closed to you and that those of earth will soon follow suit. This does not happen at once, of course, for consequences are not immediately visible on the physical plane. A decree first has to be voted in the world above, and it takes time for it to be applied in the world below. You know how these things happen in government or big business, well, it is the same in our personal lives. With their theories of liberty, young people who accept no moral or spiritual authority cut themselves off from everything that could help them. They are adrift without compass or protection of any kind, and with no notion of all the dangers, both physical and psychic, which threaten them. They lead each other on, and the result is often catastrophic.

Some of them say: 'I'd like to be able to trust a spiritual guide, but there are so many charlatans and crazy people who claim to be Masters.' That is true, but no one is asking you to follow such people. Is it rational to make the existence of a few crooks and lunatics an excuse to forget or reject the genuine benefactors of humanity? Do you refuse to listen to good music just because a few musicians produce horrible cacophonic noises? Do you never visit museums to admire the works of Leonardo Da Vinci, Rembrandt, or Michelangelo just because a few painters produce nothing but ugly daubs and gargoyles? Do you refuse to read books just because some people write all kinds of nonsense? How illogical can you be? The truth is that it is easy to listen to music, admire works of art, or read books, whereas to embark on a spiritual path, accept discipline, and behave with altruism all require a great deal of time and effort. So the lazy use every possible pretext to refuse the light of a genuine guide and avoid having to exert themselves.

You will say that it is difficult to recognize a true Master among all the charlatans and crooks who exploit people's gullibility today. No, in reality it is not difficult to recognize a true Master, on the condition, that is, that you have a very clear idea of what you are looking for. As I say, the spiritual life is a discipline which requires a great deal of time and effort, and if someone comes along and begins by promising that, as his disciple, you will obtain clairvoyance and psychic powers very

'Unless you become like children' 147

quickly and easily – it seems that some even assure you of initiation within three days – you must mistrust him. And all the more so if he asks for money – sometimes a great deal of money – in exchange for such rapid results.

The truth is that money is no use at all when it comes to achieving spiritual progress. It costs nothing to practise every day to achieve self-control, to be considerate with others, to link yourself with God through prayer and meditation... all this is free. But it all takes time, and as human beings are both lazy and impatient to achieve success, they are immediately attracted by someone who promises them miraculous results, even if the price is high. But in this case why do they complain of being swindled? When you want to find a Master you have to know what you expect of him. Those who want to delude themselves about the true nature of what they are looking for will always find someone to deceive them.

Now, if you are afraid of being deceived and defrauded by a living guide, what is to prevent you from turning to those who left the world a long time ago? Their works are here, the shelves of libraries are loaded with them, and although they express things differently, all initiates, great Masters of humanity, saints, prophets, and true mystics say the same thing. You must not imagine that when I tell you you need a guide it is because

I want you to follow me. No, I am not looking for disciples. I welcome those who come to me because I am happy to be able to help as many people as possible, but I know what it means for me, for they all come with their burdens, and those burdens are then placed on my shoulders. Do you think this is an advantage for me? I accept these burdens, but I do not go and look for them. So, if I talk to you like this, it is in the hope that each one of you will decide to follow the path of true development; that each one will find and follow the guide you trust. In every religion you can find guides to lead you to your spiritual homeland.

All human beings who have reached a certain degree of psychic maturity and are capable of providing for themselves can and should free themselves gradually from the tutelage of their parents and lead an autonomous life. But spiritual maturity is less easily acquired and takes much longer. Those who want to grow spiritually also need parents, and they need the same receptive attitude towards them as they had towards their father and mother when they were children.

Children trust their parents: they follow them and listen to them, accept their advice and imitate them. If they distrust what their parents say and always want an explanation ('Why do I have to wash? Why must I get dressed? Where are you taking me? Explain: I want to understand. Are you sure the food you give me is not poison?...') they will suffer various anomalies and normal development will be impossible. It is thanks to their trust in their parents that children grow and make progress, and one day they understand why their parents made them do certain things. They may go even further, and discover things for themselves. Well, in the spiritual sphere, human beings – even when they are adult – are in the same situation as children. They need to trust those who have gone before them on the path of light. These beings have bequeathed to humanity the immense knowledge that is the fruit of thousands of years of experience, and it is up to us now to be open to them, to accept their counsel and imitate them.

Some say: 'First of all I need indisputable proof of the existence of God and invisible entities, of the immortality of the spirit, and of life after death.' Well, such people risk having to wait a long time, a very long time. And as they will do nothing while they are waiting, they will inevitably stagnate. They will prevent their best qualities from developing and will always be unhappy. Perhaps you think it is normal to want to understand and see before committing yourself? Well, in that case you are like someone in a dark room who refuses to switch on the light until the exact functioning of the electrical system has been explained in detail. Or like one who refuses to ride in your automobile until you have dismantled the engine and explained exactly how every component works. Would it not be more sensible to begin by turning the switch or getting into the car? There will be time enough to learn how it all works later.

Now, I want to talk to you about a passage from the Gospels which Christians have not always understood correctly.

At that time the disciples came to Jesus and asked, 'Who is the greatest in the kingdom of heaven?' He called a child, whom he put among them, and said, 'Truly I tell you, unless you change and become like children, you will never enter the kingdom of heaven. Whoever becomes humble like this child is the greatest in the kingdom of heaven.'[10]

Why did Jesus give us the example of children? What is there in a child that we should imitate? Of course, as children have not had time to manifest their true nature, we can think that they are pure, innocent, and blameless, but is that really the case? When you see what they become as adults you might well doubt that they were truly pure and innocent when they were children.

So what are the qualities and virtues that make a child worthy to enter the kingdom of heaven? Children are neither particularly clean nor wise;

---

[10] Mt 18:1-3

'Unless you become like children' 151

they are careless, selfish, and capricious – all of which is normal since they are still children – so why do you think Jesus asked adults forty, fifty, or eighty years old to become like children? Nicodemus asked Jesus the same question. When Jesus said: *'No one can see the kingdom of God without being born from above,'* Nicodemus asked: *'How can anyone be born after having grown old? Can one enter a second time into the mother's womb and be born?'*[11]

If we want to grasp the true meaning of Jesus' words, we must first note that he did not say: 'if you do not remain children,' but 'if you do not become children.' These words need to be explained. An adult who remains a child is not the same as one who becomes a child. The passage from childhood to adulthood is part of our normal evolution. If cosmic intelligence has decreed that human beings should pass from childhood to adulthood and thence to old age it is for a reason, and it would not have been very sensible for Jesus to want to go against this order of things. Adults have to free themselves from the weaknesses of childhood, but having done so they have to recover the good characteristics of a child.

The most obvious characteristic of a child is trust. A child knows that it is small, and its looks

---

[11] Jn 3:3-5

and gestures arouse the tenderness and good-will of adults. What other reaction is possible in the face of that trust and dependence? So they take a child's hand in theirs. A small child has complete trust in its parents, particularly in its mother. When a stranger approaches, you will see it run to its mother's arms and hide its face in her shoulder or cling to her clothes. It knows what to do to be safe. And when it senses danger it screams, 'Mama, Mama!' Well, that is what it means to be a child, whereas adults always think that they have to rely only on themselves. This is where they are wrong.

Of course, adults are too old to take their father's or mother's hand, but how can they think they no longer need parents? Oh yes, they still need parents. On the spiritual plane we always need our parents otherwise we will be lost and unhappy, just as children are lost and unhappy when they are suddenly deprived of their physical parents. However great your knowledge and experience, you all need to recover the uncomplicated, spontaneous, open, trusting heart of a child. Then, even if you are very old, you will be accepted in the kingdom of God. Yes, when you present yourself as a child the old man or old woman will follow. The grandfather or grandmother will slip in thanks to the child.

Anyone who has ever had occasion to compare human beings and animals will have seen how

'Unless you become like children' 153

much more quickly an animal grows and reaches adulthood. Some mammals reach maturity and start to reproduce a few months or a year after birth, whereas human children... Why do human beings develop so slowly? Because the nature of men and women is so extraordinarily rich. So many physical and psychic elements have to be put in place before they are in full possession of their faculties, and until they reach this stage, they need the help and protection of their parents. But the evolution of a human being does not cease when the role of the parents is complete, for a human being is a spiritual entity who continually needs to advance and grow. The process is endless. This is why, on the spiritual plane, we will always be children, always in need of parents.

Becoming a child in order to enter the kingdom of heaven does not mean a regression to infancy. Those who want to be children, spiritually speaking, need great wisdom, and the more open they are to their heavenly parents and the more readily they allow themselves to be led by them, the greater will be the wisdom they acquire. But if you asked some people what they think about this, they would say: 'As soon as we're eighteen or twenty we are considered to be adults, and now that we've shaken off the authority of our parents, there is no question of submitting to a different authority. Now that we're free we want to make the most of our freedom. We can get along without anyone else.' And sure enough, they will make the most of their freedom... to destroy themselves.

Why are there so many suicides and accidental deaths of boys and girls between the ages of fifteen and twenty? Because these are years of great inner vulnerability. The passage from childhood to adolescence is marked by important changes, not only physical and physiological, but also psychological. A child that lived in an inner relationship of osmosis with its parents gradually sheds that state of dependence and becomes an autonomous individual. But this autonomy is not acquired overnight. It has to be built up gradually on firm foundations, and this is something that adolescents do not – and often do not want to – know.

Adolescents tend to reject the order in which they have been brought up and contest all forms of authority. Parents, teachers, society, religion are all the targets of rebellion. They want to be free, they want to decide things for themselves, but as it is impossible to live without attachments of some kind, while rejecting indiscriminately all that made up the universe of their childhood, they often attach themselves with passion to certain people or ideas. This might be a good thing if they were capable of discernment, but as their new-found enthusiasms are often as baseless as their rejections, they live

'Unless you become like children'

in a state of instability and inner insecurity. For some, who are more vulnerable or more sensitive than others, this state of affairs can have tragic consequences: alcohol, drugs, violence, accidents, and suicide.

Because adolescents do not know how to channel their energies at the very time when life is beginning to manifest most powerfully within them, they are in danger of death. And it is in this respect that the responsibility of parents is very grave. If they remembered their own experience at the same critical period, they should foresee the problem years before their children have to go through it, and be able to give them in advance the elements they need to survive these storms and earthquakes. Instead of this, what do we see? Parents are completely out of their depth. They let things slide and do nothing, telling themselves that after a difficult period everything will settle down as before. Well, in this they are exactly like animals: they leave their offspring to fend for themselves without knowing whether they will survive or not...

If I take the liberty of saying these things it is because I have been obliged to see what happens to so many young men and women whose parents have allowed them to go their own way. They reach the age of twenty or twenty-five, and instead of developing harmoniously and becoming truly adult, they still have the psychology of disoriented adolescents. I have been dumbfounded by some of the things they have told me about themselves. And what a burden of care and responsibility for me, all these young people who are so completely lost! The whole of their education needs to start all over from the beginning.

And when at last I am beginning to pull these poor creatures out of the abyss they are in, along come the parents, wringing their hands and complaining that their children have been snared by a sect. They have left them to their own resources for years and given them no help when they most needed it, and now they refuse to let anyone else help them, because what they will learn in an initiatic school does not conform to their own philosophy. What exactly do these parents want?

Well, I will say no more... For me this is simply an occupational hazard. And I know that the situation in which parents find themselves is also very difficult. They cannot always be sure who their children are associating with or how they are being influenced by school and society. Many parents too have asked me to help them to set their children free from an addiction to drugs or delinquent behavior. My job is not to side with parents against their children, or with children against their parents, but simply to help them to understand certain laws of psychic life.

So to all of you, young and not so young, I say this: 'Whether you are adolescents or adults, even though you no longer need to be guided by your physical parents, you all need to accept the guidance and protection of your spiritual parents, your heavenly Father and divine Mother. That is what Jesus meant when he said: *'Unless you change and become like children, you will never enter the kingdom of heaven.'*

We must all look with confidence to those who have gone farther on the way of light – all the initiates and the great Masters – for they can help and guide us. You never need fear that they will abuse their authority by depriving you of your freedom: they have no desire to keep you for themselves. Their sole aim is to put you in touch with a world to which you could not immediately have access by yourselves. Currents of pure energy flow through such beings; they are like springs at which you can quench your thirst until such time as you can drink directly from the cosmic source.

Just as good parents know that that they must not keep their children for themselves, a spiritual Master knows that his only task is to prepare you for your divine parents, that is, for the parents of your soul and spirit: the Universal Soul and the Cosmic Spirit. You have sometimes laughed when I said that I see myself simply as a signpost, but this is only another way of saying the same thing:

like your parents, my responsibility is to point you in the right direction, in the direction of your heavenly homeland.

Chapter Nine

'THE GREATEST OF THESE IS LOVE'

The natural tendency of those who discover faith is to want to share it immediately with others. They feel that they have found truth, they have found salvation, and something tells them that they must convey that faith and that salvation to everyone. So whenever they can buttonhole someone they start preaching and sermonizing, convinced that since they are only doing it for his good, he should at least listen. Well, let me tell you, this reveals a very poor understanding of people's psychology.

However enthusiastic you may feel about your new-found religion or spiritual teaching you must not begin by preaching it to others. First, because people are fed up with sermons; they no longer believe in them. The only thing that carries conviction is example, the way you express your faith in your behavior. Second, because to start talking about your faith at once shows a poor knowledge of your own psychology as well. Faith is something that has to be lived in the deepest part of your being so that what you believe may become your own flesh and blood. If you start proclaiming it right away, something within you will crumble, and at the first obstacle, the slightest jolt, your faith will be shaken. Very soon, even though you may cling to certain principles and dogmas, they will not correspond to something vital within you; you will dry up and become rigid, because the springs of faith will have ceased to flow.

We have to find very subtle ways of expressing our faith, otherwise we will lose it or, worse still, it will soon become fanaticism. And those subtle ways can only be inspired by love. For love is greater than faith. This is what St Paul said in his first epistle to the Corinthians.

If I have prophetic powers, and understand all mysteries and all knowledge, and if I have all faith, so as to remove mountains, but do not have love, I am nothing... And now faith, hope, and love abide, these three; and the greatest of these is love.[12]

To love God is more important than to have faith in him. You will perhaps say that both have done a great deal of damage. That is true. There have always been fanatics who did not hesitate to chop off the heads of so-called pagans, miscreants,

---

[12] Cor 13:2,13

infidels, or heretics in the name of their love of God, thinking that this would please him. If they massacred so many, it was because they believed their souls to be sunk in darkness and sin and a constant affront to God. By expediting their departure for the next world they saved them from persisting in their erroneous ways. So many atrocities have been committed in the name of the love of God that those who speak of that love are more and more likely to be regarded with suspicion. People today consider that we should turn our attention to human beings and forget about that remote and imaginary Deity who was no more than a pretext to persecute others.

But the truth is that if we do not begin by learning to love God we will never know how to love human beings, we will only harm them, because our love will be neither intelligent nor enlightened. We should not put too much trust in what the human heart tells us, for although that heart contains many good things, it also contains greed, violence, self-interest, possessiveness, and jealousy. Yes, the human heart is a dark pit which conceals every kind of monster. It needs to be purified and enlightened, and we cannot do this unless we learn to turn to the Creator. Even when our concern is for creatures, we cannot maintain the right orientation if we do not also remember the Creator.

It is not only those who preach the love of God who are guilty. Those who preach the love of humanity have also committed very grave faults, and atheists have slaughtered their fellow human beings just as savagely as believers. There is no need to quote chapter and verse: the examples of countries subject to political regimes determined to wipe out every form of religion and spirituality is sufficiently eloquent. The inhabitants are no freer and no happier than before. So it is not religion that is to blame. The fault lies with human beings who refuse to see any need to look for and practise the best methods of self-improvement. This is why they spoil everything they touch, not only religion, but also philosophy, politics, science, the arts, and so on. Each of these becomes only what human beings have made of them.

Instead of asking whether it is better to love God or to love human beings, it would be more to the point to make up your minds to do some inner work. Those who do not consider this work to have priority have no choice but to manifest as malevolent beings. Whether in their family or in society they can do only harm. This is why I keep telling you that the one question you need to be absolutely clear about is that of the two natures, the higher and the lower, which together constitute a human being.

When you first meet a man, you should not imagine that you will know much about him when you learn that he is a bishop, a prince, a president, a minister, a professor, a doctor, a lawyer, the CEO of a company, a laborer, or a peasant... And you will be none the wiser when you learn whether he is married or not, whether he has children or not. His social position is no guarantee of how he will behave. The only concern of our lower nature is to find the sphere in which it can most easily manifest its need to dominate, satisfy its passions, and fulfil its ambitions, and these conditions may be found equally in the activities of a bishop, of a businessman, or of anyone else. Those who have never worked to achieve the mastery of their lower nature cannot claim to know what love is: they love neither God nor their fellow humans.

Love is a cosmic force which impregnates the totality of our psychic being. In human beings it takes different forms depending on whether it manifests primarily through the mind, the heart, or the will, and then it is known in turn as indulgence, kindness, or charity. These manifestations of love come from different sources which – as we will see – are related but not identical.

Although indulgence is a virtue which pertains to the heart, it is strongly influenced by the mind. Only those who are truly intelligent can be indulgent. Why? Because when you have a keen understanding of what human beings are and of the various factors which constitute their underlying nature, when you see how the environment in which they live can influence their behavior, and when you recognize the difficulties they are up against, you cannot judge them too harshly even though they may behave very badly. You can be lucid about them, for lucidity is one of the attributes of the mind, but you can also be more tolerant, more understanding. Those who possess certain attributes of the heart but who are narrow-minded and have little intelligence can soon become aggressive, intolerant, and unfeeling. Nothing reveals a lack of intelligence more clearly than the absence of indulgence, which is a lack of understanding.

History tells us how Christians filled with the love of God – and even of charity toward their fellow humans – persecuted, imprisoned, and burned so many very pure and noble beings, whereas others, who were perhaps not so full of love, behaved with tolerance, respect and kindness because they were intelligent. You will perhaps say: 'But people with a highly developed intellect also have a strong critical sense and are not usually particularly indulgent. In fact, they can be very cruel.' Well, this means that they lack true intelligence. As people come to understand things better and have a broader view of reality, they become more intelligent and more indulgent.

Kindness, for its part, is influenced more by the heart than by the mind, and this is why it is often said that kind people are not very bright. They are so eager to help others that they are inclined to be naïve and gullible. But kindness also has strong ties to the will. Kind people always feel the need to manifest their kindness in deeds: they exert themselves to support and help others; they will sometimes shake people out of their difficulties; a rough exterior often hides a very kind heart. But although it is not a quality of the mind, kindness, even more than indulgence, represents a form of intelligence, for it is not content to spare others, it goes out of its way to help them. Those who devote their mental faculties, their time, and their strength to helping their fellow human beings are the most intelligent, for true intelligence is to forget oneself in the service of others.

And what about charity? Well, charity should be the expression of the highest degree of love, for together with faith and hope it is called a 'theological virtue', that is, a virtue whose object is God. Originally, the word charity designated the love of a human being for God, which necessarily gave rise to the love of neighbor: human beings who love God must also love him through their neighbors. Unfortunately, over the centuries the word charity has lost its sublime connotation, and what is known as charity today usually refers to actions which may express no true feelings of any kind. Many people perform 'deeds of charity' because the Church and their families taught them to give to the poor and comfort the sorrowful. So they give away their cast-offs or a few pennies in alms, and their consciences are at ease. Well, that has nothing to do with kindness.

Even though kindness is expressed in actions, it goes further than that. Many successive incarnations are necessary in order to develop this virtue to the full, whereas charity is often the product of a brief education. So many people make the lives of their children or of their friends and relations miserable because of their so-called 'charity'. They may give a great deal of money to the Church and other good works, but they make themselves detestable. It is possible to meet many people who are charitable but not very many who are truly kind.

So indulgence, kindness, and charity are all aspects of love, but we still do not know what true love is. True love concerns the whole being, and only those who work at the harmonious development of their mind, heart, and will can know love, feel love, live in love, and give love. True love is a state of consciousness, the highest state of consciousness that can be attained by a

'The greatest of these is love'

human being. It is the fullness of divine consciousness. Those who are touched by that love – if only for a brief instant – feel almost as though they had been struck by lightning. The sensation is so beautiful, so sublime, that they cannot bear it, but it is this love that enlightens, vivifies, and resuscitates. Of course, this state of consciousness has nothing in common with what we usually mean by love, which is often no more than an untidy welter of feelings.

It is easier to believe than to love. Faith does not require you to open your heart to others, to work, to take the first step toward them, to make sacrifices for them. When you believe, you can be proud of your convictions and fight tooth and nail to defend them. There is nothing to oblige you to be understanding or to show sympathy, consideration, or devotion in your dealings with other human beings. Looking at history we see not only that religion has been the cause of all kinds of horrors and atrocities, but that those who committed these horrors were persuaded that they were doing their duty. To imprison and massacre 'heretics' and 'infidels' with no scruples about the inhumanity of such behavior was simply a proof of faith. Many, indeed, would have said they were acting out of brotherly love, for by burning people at the stake they were saving them from the fires of hell and eternal damnation. It is amazing to see what madness fanaticism engendered in some Christians. And they were sure that God would reward them for their good deeds. But I wonder: did they ever ask God whether he approved the massacre of his creatures?

This is the first question that today's 'champions of the faith' should ask themselves. They consider themselves to be instruments of the divine will, but in reality no one can be an authentic instrument of God's will before having learned and achieved a great deal. Too many people take their own will for the will of God. An idea or desire suddenly occurs to them, a conviction starts them off in this direction or that, and there you are: they are carrying out what they suppose to be God's will. But if you want to know and become an instrument of his will, you need to work tirelessly to free yourself from your own weaknesses and limitations. How could God speak and make known his will to such imperfect instruments? You have to understand that the cosmic law of affinity applies here, too. Human beings can make contact only with the entities and currents that correspond to what is in them, and many of those who think they are serving God are in reality serving entities of darkness.

For Christians who want to become the instruments of divine will there is only one thing to do: live according to Jesus' teaching as we find

'The greatest of these is love'

it in the Gospels. What he said was very clear and simple. Take, for instance, these words: *You shall love the Lord your God with all your heart, with all your soul, with all your mind, and with all your strength... And you shall love your neighbor as yourself.* [13] Those who work sincerely to put God at the center of their lives and who learn to deal honestly, kindly, and with indulgence with their fellow humans can hope one day to become instruments of the divine will. Until then they would be deluding themselves. As long as they have not purified themselves, as long as their inner life is still in disorder, they cannot be instruments of the divine will but only of the demons which constantly seek to enter human beings.

The truth is that fanatics are not true believers. If they are incapable of respecting the faith of others, it is because they have not understood on what principles their own faith should be based. This reminds me of an episode of my youth. Whenever possible, I would climb Mount Musallah, and one day as I was on my way down, I saw a man coming toward me. We had barely said good day before he took a book from his pocket. It was a Bible, and he read a few verses which he then commented in an aggressive tone of voice with furious glances in my direction. Of course,

---

[13] Mt 22:37

the passage he had chosen spoke of divine wrath and punishment. At one point he told me that he was a Protestant minister... It was not necessary to tell me: I had suspected as much right away.

Well, I began by listening patiently. I cannot remember now exactly what he said but I do remember that it had to do with faith, sin, and eternal damnation. The thing I remember most clearly is that it was very cold, for Mount Musallah is very high and we were at an altitude of about three thousand meters. Anyway, after a while I was tired of his threatening discourse, so I interrupted him: 'Reverend sir, I have been listening to you, and since you are a minister, I must tell you that if you had read the Gospels more attentively you would not stand there casting fire and brimstone on me and all other unfortunate human beings. You would like me to believe that there is nothing greater than the Bible, in the name of which – according to your faith – you would be ready to sacrifice the whole human race. Well, let me tell you that if I had to choose between your Bible and you, I would throw this Bible over the edge of the precipice, whereas I would do everything in my power to keep you safe and well, for you are a living Bible.'

I cannot describe to you the expression of amazement on his face. Of course, he was scandalized by what I had said, but at the same

'The greatest of these is love'

time he must have been pleased too, for he softened his tone of voice. He must have thought to himself: 'Ah, at least he must really value me if he would choose to save me rather than the Bible.' He had just learned that he was a living Bible. Then, when I saw that he was trembling – whether with cold or for other reasons, I do not know – I poured some hot water from my thermos, and gave it to him, saying: 'Here, have a drink.' He took the cup and began to drink. He took a sip... then he looked at me... another sip... and another look... And I drank too and the situation relaxed. So, now you know about my conversation with a clergyman who imagined he was fulfilling his mission when he threatened me in the name of the Bible.

The word 'bible' means book. But the only true book is the great book of living nature, the book, that is, of the universe created by God and of the human beings made in the image of that universe, into whom God breathed his own spirit. Every sacred book has its origins in this one great book of which it represents no more than a few fragments. Only the great book of nature is complete and indestructible, and if you do not learn to read it, you could spend your entire life reading the Bible and still not understand very much. Fanatics may brandish the Bible, the Koran, or other sacred scriptures, but however genuinely inspired those scriptures may be, they can never substitute for the one book in which the Creator has written everything: a human being. This 'book' possesses what none of the sacred texts possesses: a living, immortal soul and spirit.

If theologians are unable to decipher the Bible correctly it is because they have never uncovered the mysteries of a human being. Of course, if they heard me they would protest and want to argue about it. But I do not have time to argue, I only know that if sacred scriptures exist it is because there have been human beings capable of interpreting the spiritual realities they discovered in themselves and in the universe.

Human beings are strange creatures: they take pride and boast about all kinds of insignificant details while remaining unaware of what makes them so precious, unique, and irreplaceable. The fact that the Creator made them in his own image, and that they contain all the wonders of heaven and earth does not really interest them. But a book? Ah, that is worth something! They have massacred millions of their fellow human beings for the sake of a book.

The sacred scriptures of all religions are very precious – I am certainly not the one to deny that – but human beings are far more precious, because they are alive and possess the whole of the universe within them. Why save printed books and persecute true, living books? Perhaps you think

'The greatest of these is love'

that if the sacred scriptures disappeared there would be no way of finding truth. But there is no danger: they can always be restored, for their source is on a higher plane, in the zodiac, in the stars, and in human beings. But theologians do not understand this; their only concern is to study, and compare, and comment the texts. They need to look beyond their texts, to look higher and further, to look at life. If they did this they would understand better. Texts are static, they are there and they never change, but life evolves and human beings need other kinds of nourishment. Exegesis is certainly interesting – intellectually interesting – but it is not really very useful for our spiritual life.

Faith without love engenders fanaticism, and this is the worst thing that can happen to human beings, because it drives them mad and makes monsters of them. The name of God is always on their lips and they are ready to annihilate the whole world for his glory. But when they are in the midst of tribulations, when they are the victims of disasters such as epidemics, floods, earthquakes, famine, and so on, who is it that comes to their rescue? Non-believers. Yes, because believers are too busy mumbling their prayers, asking God to help the victims. Or, worse still, they interpret these misfortunes as a divine punishment and glory in the sight of God's wrath striking down the wicked.

Yes, it makes you wonder what germ of callousness is contained in faith. It is often the spectacle of believers that discourages others from believing. Their narrow viewpoint locks them into their religion and offers a monstrous, repugnant picture of the Deity. And yet they do not hesitate to say that God is love. They have been told that and they repeat it. Well, they are going to have to make a deal of progress if they want us to believe that their God is love.

Faith and love are not in principle two separate worlds: they are linked and mutually supportive. But as long as true faith is not correctly understood, there can be no real love. And vice versa: as long as you are incapable of manifesting love you cannot claim to have faith. It is right to have faith and to stand up for it, but it is wrong to try to force it on others. In fact that is no longer faith but fanaticism.

Many people think that having found faith they have a duty to go out and preach it to the world. This is a mistake, because, in the first place, truths are subjective. Even though all human beings are identical in structure – they all have a spirit, a soul, a mind, a heart, and a will – their sensibilities, their understanding, their needs, and their aspirations are all different, so they cannot all perceive things in the same way. The arguments they have among themselves, when each one claims to possess truth,

'The greatest of these is love'

are quite senseless. Perhaps you say: 'But does this mean there is no such thing as truth?' No, truth exists all right! The more we raise our inner life to higher levels, the more we detach ourselves from our petty self-interests and purify ourselves, the more divine light fills us and the closer we come to truth. But it is impossible to say whether or not anyone will ever know truth as an absolute principle. The only thing we can say with any certainty is that by gradually stripping away the opaque layers built up around us by our dark and unruly thoughts and feelings we come closer to it. And when this is the case, we no longer feel the need to preach to others or to combat them.

Truth will never force itself on us as something self-evident, less still as something we must force on others. It is we ourselves, through an orderly and rational psychic life who become capable of finding the truth... although we may never actually manage to find it. Truth is simply the result of our capacity for self-perfection. This means that many people should stop priding themselves on belonging to the only true religion. It is not their baptism certificate that counts, it is the efforts they make day after day to conquer their weaknesses. That is the only indication that they belong to the true religion.

Believers must get rid of the illusion that their beliefs are articles of faith which are valid for all.

If you decide to follow a spiritual teaching, instead of talking to everybody about it try to practise it reasonably and leave other people in peace. This precaution is particularly useful when you are still a beginner, for it takes time to be inwardly strong and well armed. It is never very easy to understand exactly what spirituality is, and this means that those who do not begin by being perfectly sincere with themselves can sometimes slip into deviant behavior.

On the pretext of being detached from material things, some 'spiritualists' fall into the opposite excesses to the point of defying all the laws of hygiene, esthetics, and even common sense. As though the spirit could enjoy living in dirt, ugliness, and insanity! You will say: 'But there have been ascetics...' Well, I am not so sure that all those who have claimed to be ascetics had really come close to the spirit. A taste for privations can be pathological. There are people who enjoy being ill-treated and made to suffer, just as others enjoy pleasure, but it is not a proof of spirituality.

Now I want to say something about a rather sensitive question. Those who decide to follow a spiritual teaching, sensing that it is the way for them, are going to have to change many of their mental patterns and their habits in life. This is not always easy, especially because they are not the only ones concerned: the habits of their family, friends, neighbors, or colleagues will also be affected and they may object. So what is to be done? When you find yourself in this situation – it will always be inevitable to some degree – you must make it clear that you understand that love is greater than faith. As far as it is possible, you must not cause others to suffer, and of course, you must not abandon them.

If your behavior is excessive and fanatical, if you try to force your spirituality on others, and as a result they become aggressive and more materialistic than ever, the responsibility will be yours. If you show understanding and patience you may get them to accept your new way of life, whereas if you are intransigent not only will you fail to convince them, but they will become even more critical, hostile, even vindictive, and you will find yourself embroiled in such complications that you will be led to make some serious mistakes.

There is no separation between our faith, our beliefs, and our daily lives, and this means that things are always more complicated than we imagine. When you decide to embrace a religion or a spiritual philosophy and to put its principles into practice in your life, not only will you encounter difficulties with yourself because of the efforts required of you, but you will also have difficulties with others who will not necessarily understand how and why you have changed. Well, it is these difficulties and the way you handle them which will reveal the quality, the authenticity of your faith. It is not enough to say, for example, 'Now that I know the teaching of the Universal White Brotherhood, I'm going to change my life completely, and I don't care what the family thinks. If it makes them unhappy, or hostile, or furious that's not my problem.' Oh but it is your problem, because your spiritual life will depend on how you resolve it.

Our inner life is built on the twin pillars of faith and love, and we have to work at them both. There are scientists who would eliminate faith, saying that they want to free us from all those superstitions. And there are philosophers who despise love. They see a form of weakness and servility in some of its manifestations such as kindness, gentleness, or humility, and would have us develop only the mind. Well, all this promises conflicts ahead. I am no antagonist of either science or philosophy, but I can see that the two pillars of our inner temple have been badly shaken, and if we do nothing to strengthen them again the whole edifice will collapse. When faith and love no longer exist how can we speak of hope?

In order to avoid the errors and excesses of faith we must never separate it from love. On the contrary, we must make it subject to love, for love is always greater than faith. Once we understand

'The greatest of these is love'

this we no longer need to ask whom we should love: God or human beings? We love God and we love human beings because the love of human beings results from love of God. This is the meaning of the answer Jesus gave to the scribe who asked: 'Which commandment in the law is the greatest?' Jesus said:

You shall love the Lord your God with all your heart, with all your soul, with all your mind. This is the greatest and first commandment. And a second is like it: you shall love your neighbor as yourself. On these two commandments hang all the law and the prophets.[14]

So it is useless to argue or shilly-shally. If you do not love God first there will always be something missing in the way you love your neighbor.

You will perhaps ask: 'But how can I know if I truly love and believe in God?' That is easy: if you love and believe in him you will be grateful to him and think of thanking him. Most people do exactly the opposite. They say they believe in God and imagine they love him, but their faith and their love is usually manifested only in demands. They think that God is there to watch over them and protect them; he should give them what they ask for – and let him look out if he does not do so: they

---

[14] Mt 22:36-40

will stop loving or believing in him! Oh yes, that is the faith and love of many 'believers': it is all demands and recriminations. No wonder their faith is so shaky and their love so changeable.

To most human beings love is a question of asking, of clamoring for something. Yes, truly: this is how they interpret it. This is how they behave towards God as well as towards the people they claim to love. They pursue them with their demands and are always dissatisfied, however much they receive. So here again is the criterion. Do you want to know whether you love human beings? It is simple: ask yourself whether you are grateful to them. If you do not want anything from them, if you feel like thanking them – in words or simply in your thoughts – for being there, for existing, then, yes, you can be sure that you love them. If not, call your feeling for them what you please, but it is not love.

A great light will dawn in the consciousness of human beings the day they learn to thank God in any and every circumstance. To thank him for what he gives them and for what he holds from them. It is through gratitude that they will achieve the state of consciousness in which faith and love are one. When they reach this level, their love of God will necessarily be beneficial for human beings. If your days and nights are spent in giving thanks to God and his creatures, there will be no room in your head or your heart for fanaticism.

'The greatest of these is love'

There are all kinds of books which explain how to meditate, which give you formulas to repeat during your meditations, and so on. I do not deny that they can be useful and effective, but there is one word which is never mentioned. A word which, to my mind, is more powerful than any other. A word which enlightens, harmonizes, and heals: the word 'Thanks!'. I have tried many different methods in my lifetime. I have made a great many experiments, but as soon as I adopted the habit of consciously saying 'Thanks!' I sensed that I was holding a magic wand capable of transforming everything. Oh of course, you will say in disappointment: 'But that's nothing!' No, I know that if I gave you a Tibetan formula – if only the word 'OM' – your curiosity would immediately be aroused. Well, the formula I give you is simply 'Thanks!'. Thanks, thanks, thanks... and if you know how to say this word, its work within you will reach to the very marrow of your bones.

Nothing is more important than to thank God: 'Thank you God, I thank you with my whole heart, my whole mind, my whole soul, and my whole spirit. Thank you!' You will have all of eternity in which to see the great value of this word. You cannot expect to see it in a week or two. Repeat it as often as you can, and one day you will realize that it is worth more than gold.

Chapter Ten

BASE YOUR TRUST ON VIGILANCE

The human need to believe not only in something but in someone expresses itself in many different ways. When people are unable or unwilling to believe in God, they tend to make a deity of the man or woman they love, of the king, queen, or president of their country, of an artist, a philosopher, a scientist... or a soccer star. You will say that I am exaggerating: people do not really make deities of them. No? Well, what would you call it when people place all their hopes in someone, when their joy and happiness, the solution of their material problems, the very meaning of their lives are conditioned by this person – until, of course, they discover they have been deluding themselves?

But is it such a bad thing to have illusions about people? No, for it is often our illusions that make life possible. Until we are capable of understanding and feeling that God the Creator of the universe is the only one worthy of absolute trust, we need to have different experiences, both happy and unhappy, for that is how we learn.

If a man tells his wife he loves her and is generous with his gifts, she will be happy in the belief that he is faithful to her, when all the time he has a mistress – and perhaps more than one! So which is better: that she should learn the truth and be devastated by it, or that she should continue to be happy in her illusions? I cannot judge, it depends on the persons concerned. Experiences which would destroy some people can be an occasion for others to become stronger. I will say, simply, that whoever is concerned, and whatever their level of inner evolution, their task is to make use of every experience for their instruction and growth in perfection.

Human beings are obliged, whether they like it or not, to live with others. They depend on others, and a relationship with others is possible only if there is a minimum of mutual trust. Think of how it is when you drive: if you started worrying about whether the other drivers on the highway were careful, safe, and sober you would never get anywhere. No, without realizing it you trust them. And it is the same when you travel by train or plane: you trust the driver or pilot. When you want to buy food at the grocery store, do you stand outside for half-an-hour trying to decide whether

Base your trust on vigilance 189

you should go in, because, you never know, they might be selling something poisonous? No, trust is so natural that you do not even realize it exists. This is what makes life in society possible: every business enterprise, all commerce, every commitment is a proof of trust.

Think of the many daily gestures which presuppose a situation of trust. If someone hands you something, you trust him not to drop it before you have hold of it. If someone opens a door and gestures to you to go ahead of him, you trust him not to push past you or try to slam it in your face. When you start to do something, others trust you not to change your mind at the last moment. If, for instance, you start to cross the road and then hesitate in the middle and want to turn back, you are liable to cause an accident, because the people driving automobiles having seen you, trusted you to continue. Once you had started across the road they counted on your going all the way. Well, each of these examples can be transposed onto other levels of existence.

Trust is operative from the first moment of waking in the morning. You need to face the day with trust. If you had to leave your house in the morning thinking that someone might attack you or a car might run over you, that a flower pot might fall from a window and knock you out, your life would be hell. Even the most distrustful people are obliged to have a minimum of trust. Life is founded on trust, on faith.

Now, do not misunderstand me: I am not saying you can go through life with your eyes closed, trusting every single person. The question is more complicated than that, and this is why we continually meet people who complain that they have been deceived and misled, that their trust has been abused. Why is this? Because they have not yet understood that other people's response to their trust depends on what they are, on their experience of life and the lessons they have drawn from it.

If you do not know how to choose the people in whom to trust, those you wish to associate with or from whom you seek advice, you need not be surprised if your expectations are disappointed. Do you feel betrayed, cheated? Well, those people were well-intentioned, they did not want to cheat or betray you, they simply acted according to their own abilities and possibilities, and it is not their fault if they failed to fulfil your expectations. It was up to you to be more clear-sighted, to reflect before pinning all your hopes on them.

You will say that you need someone to support you, to love and help you. Yes, that is normal, but that does not mean you should trust the first person who seems to be more or less what you are looking for. You must understand once and for all that you will never meet anyone who is exactly what you

Base your trust on vigilance

are looking for. If you need friends and advisers, you must at least learn to choose them wisely. Human beings are what they are: it is unwise to expect more from them than they are capable of giving... and it is even more unwise to blame them for not giving it.

I repeat: it is up to you to open your eyes, to study people and see whom you can trust. There are people to whom you can trust almost any task and it will always be done; there are those to whom you can entrust your house or even your purse, and you know that they will not touch them; there are others again to whom you can confide your worries and even your most intimate secrets, and you know they will never betray you. It is up to you to know what you can expect of each one. If you are blinded by your own needs and wishes, you cannot be clear-sighted, and in this case you need not be astonished if you are disillusioned.

So many people are dejected because they feel betrayed. They keep repeating: 'But how is it possible? He promised... She swore to me...' Yes, of course, they had been promised great things but they should not have been so naive. Most men and women are like children: they make promises which they think they are going to honor. When they make them they are sincere, convinced that they are going to do what they say, but they do not know themselves, they do not realize how weak and inadequate they are, and when the time comes they waver and betray their promises. This is only normal and you should have known it in advance. You must never ask people for something that they do not have the power to give. Or if you do so, it must be only to give them an opportunity to transcend themselves, but you must know what you are asking and what to expect, for with the best will in the world they may not be able to do what you ask.

Before relying on anyone's fidelity, begin by asking yourself who he is and whether he will always be up to it. And if he lets you down, blame only yourself. What makes you think that Providence will bring you face to face with exactly the person of your dreams? A woman meets a man, and while she is building castles in Spain, he, behind his ardent looks, his smiles, and his smooth promises, is instinctively calculating exactly how he can exploit this innocent who believes every word he says. And many men can also be victims. It is not only in affairs of the heart that misadventures of this kind occur: business, politics, the whole of life in society is strewn with broken promises. It is almost impossible not to be let down at some time or another, but at least you must learn from the experience.

There are people who, however many disappointments they encounter, remain obstinately trusting. They realize they have already been

Base your trust on vigilance

betrayed but it is as though they forgot and fell into the trap again. Why? It seems that they fail to learn from experience. It is as though there were no continuity in their psychic life, as though the lesson learned from one disappointment were useless for the next experience. Every time it happens, they weep and lament and swear they will never be caught out again. But as no two situations look exactly the same, they are taken in. They think that this time it will be different, that at last they have found what they were looking for, and so they are deceived once again. Others react differently: having been deceived once they refuse to trust anyone ever again, and that is no better. 'Well, what can we do?' you will ask; 'How can we know whom to trust?'

Well, if that is your question, I must tell you that it is the wrong one. As I never stop saying, human beings are composed of two natures, a higher nature and a lower nature. If someone has betrayed you it means that you have not been lucid and clear-sighted: you put your trust in his lower nature. But why this lack of lucidity? Most certainly because your trust was inspired by your own lower nature. Think about it honestly: what were you hoping for from that person? That he should help you to become a better person, wiser, and with a higher standard for yourself? Or were you not rather hoping that he would fulfil your need for pleasure and comfort, that he would satisfy your appetites, your ambition, and your baser tendencies?

Do you want the love of a man or a woman? You may get it, but if that love is primarily sensual, it will not last. Why? Because the Creator has not bestowed longevity on feelings inspired by our instincts: they are too crude, unstable, and perishable, and if that is what you are counting on you can expect to be disappointed. Only the manifestations of your higher nature, of the Deity that dwells in each human being, will never disappoint you. You would do well to distrust purely human or animal manifestations. So as you see, trust is very useful, but so is distrust: each in its rightful place can do wonders. Unfortunately human beings are more inclined to trust their business partner or their banker and to distrust God. When your banker speaks, naturally, you must listen to the wise and precious advice he gives you. But when God speaks... Pooh! Who cares?

So it all depends on you: as long as it is your lower nature that wants something from others, you must expect the response to come from their lower nature. And it will respond in its own characteristic manner, with self-interest, deceit, betrayal, and disloyalty. Of course, this will mean suffering for you, but remember that it is your lower nature that suffers. Your higher nature

Base your trust on vigilance

remains unscathed. In fact it is amused and even applauds what is happening because you will have received the lesson you deserved.

However, it can also happen that it is your divine nature which attempts to contact the divine nature of another only to be rebuffed by a hurtful or ungrateful response from that person's lower nature. Of course, you will be disappointed, but your disappointment will not go very deep, because your divine self is invulnerable to wounds of this kind. And above all, since we also receive the good as well as the evil we do to others, the good you wished to do and which was rejected will remain with you, in you. It will become a breastplate to protect you against attack.

Perhaps you understand better now how to formulate your question. You must not ask whether you can trust others and – depending on whether you are an optimist or a pessimist – answer yes or no, for the answer to this question is not a question of temperament. You can trust others when you manage to contact their higher nature, but you must expect the worst if it is their lower nature which responds. The important thing, therefore, is to have the discernment that makes this possible... And now you will be wondering how to acquire this discernment.

Many years ago I talked to you about an inner sample. Let us begin with a very simple example.

Suppose you have painted the walls of your bedroom and want to buy material for the curtains. As, of course, you want the colors to match, you daub some of the paint you used for the walls onto a small piece of wood, and then, even if the shopkeeper or anyone else tries to persuade you to buy something they like, you will look at the sample you prepared and will be able to choose something suitable. The sample will be your frame of reference.

You know all that, of course, but when it comes to discerning the nature of people or events, what frame of reference do you have? You will say that questions which concern the way we live cannot be answered as easily as the choice of paint or curtain material. That is true, of course, but it was only an analogy to help you to understand this. All human souls come from the bosom of the Almighty and they all possess an inner sample, a yardstick of true wisdom, true love, true beauty, true justice, and so on. But as most human beings have never learned to look for and cultivate these heavenly samples, they remain buried under layers and layers of false opinions, flawed points of view, and degenerate tastes. They should not be surprised, then, if having no reliable criteria to guide them, they continually make the wrong choices.

'But,' you will ask; 'How can we find this inner sample again?' First by studying the life and

Base your trust on vigilance

teaching of those who have been examples of wisdom, integrity, kindness, justice, altruism, and self-sacrifice, and by linking ourselves to them. At the same time we need to look into the depths of our own being in order to find the light that we can hardly see any more. By means of reflection, prayer, meditation, and a life of discipline we can penetrate all the opaque layers within until we recover this, the only light that can show us which choices to make. Each one of us has this inner yardstick of good, of justice, of beauty, and we must know this and know that it is also true for others. Once you are fully conscious of this truth, there will no longer be any danger of leading other people – or of being led by others – into disorder and darkness. You will help each other to follow the path of heaven.

Now, don't come and complain – as some have done – that you tried to follow my advice to be open to others, and that as a result you have been deceived, betrayed, and ill-treated. Oh yes, it is always my fault! But have I ever said you should be blind? No. So when you see someone who is unjust, dishonest, or cruel, you must not turn a blind eye, saying that since you must show trust, you should not see his faults. On the contrary, you should keep your eyes wide open and refuse to delude yourself, while trying at the same time, by your attitude, to neutralize that person's negative manifestations and even to awaken the manifestations of his divine nature. Genuine trust is based not on blindness but on vigilance.

The only way to ensure correct relations with others is never to lose sight of the existence of these two natures, the higher and the lower. Trust only the higher, divine nature both in yourself and in others. A human being is like a bank in which you invest capital. So be careful: make sure that the bank is sound and reliable, otherwise you will risk losing all you possess. And as you too are a bank, try to be a trustworthy one. The question is not only whether you can trust others, you must also ask yourself whether they can trust you. And try to be worthy of their trust. This is what you should really care about.

Now let me add just this: you may be the victim of grave injustices on the part of others, they may humiliate and ill-treat you so grievously that you lose all self-confidence. If you are truly not guilty, do everything in your power to defend yourself inwardly. What does it matter to you what such blind people think of you? They may slander, and judge, and condemn you, but why take their opinion so much to heart? Why give them the last word? If you are blameless it should be enough for you to listen to the judgement of your own inner tribunal, to your conscience, to the indwelling Deity, and let those people think and say what they

Base your trust on vigilance

please. The only thing you need to do is take care that their poison does not filter into your heart and soul.

If other human beings appreciate the good things you do, that is fine; but if they do not, never give them the chance to destroy you. Take care, above all, to be lucid about yourself, to be always honest and altruistic. Tell yourself also that your worth and your honor are not conditioned by other people's opinion of you. Your divine nature sustains you, and that should be enough for you to take courage and continue to advance.

Chapter Eleven

'AS I HAVE LOVED YOU'

'I've lost all my illusions!' How often have I heard people say that! They believed in justice, in honesty, friendship, and love, and then they were deceived, and the deception wrought such havoc within them that they lost not only their illusions, but their faith as well. Yes, many people confuse faith and illusions. It would often be to our advantage to lose our illusions, but to lose our faith in life and in human beings... how can we persuade people that this is the only true loss? Can there be any worse loss than to lose your light, to shrivel and dry up, to lose all enthusiasm, all spontaneity?

Whatever comes you must hold on to faith. I have often been struck by the faces of people who have had to confront the scheming and treachery of those around them: their eyes and their expression manifest the richness of their inner life. They have lost nothing, or rather – to use the image of the bank again – they may have lost the interest but their capital is intact. Yes, compare those who allow themselves to be devoured by disillusionment and those who continue to trust. What a difference! The former have lost their true treasure while the others have received a hundredfold, a thousandfold: they are vibrant and alive, always eager to get back to work.

I cannot find words strong enough to convey to you how important it is to hold onto the treasure of faith so that it will always be an open door. Get into the habit of weighing things on your spiritual scales. When someone has insulted you or done you an injustice, take a good look at the pros and cons of the situation, and you will see that by holding onto your faith you will gain a thousand times more than the loss inflicted by some stupid or vindictive individual. The living faith at work within you gives you life every second of your existence. It is like a ceaseless tide of crystalline water. Why deprive yourself of its blessings simply because you may sometimes suffer injury or betrayal?

Wisdom has its own special way of calculating things. It does not cut off the supply of what is indispensable, vital, and eternal just because something disagreeable happens. If you are betrayed it is only from time to time, so is it really worth depriving yourself forever of all that faith can give you? The day may come when your faith may even win over those who betrayed you – on

'As I have loved you'

the condition, of course, that you never cease to see the Deity dwelling within them, for it is this Deity alone that can be trusted.

The Master Peter Deunov once said: 'I know who betrayed me, but I continue to have faith in them because I have faith in the good in people. However feeble his good will may be, I continue to believe that it will triumph in the end. However long someone persists in deceiving me, I have faith that a true human being will one day emerge. In this way I am looking on him exactly as God looks on him. Even though all reject him and stop believing in him, God remains by his side to tell him: "It does not matter how crooked your ways have been up to now, for you can always straighten up. You will advance and a true man will emerge from you." And in the end this is what happens.'

You heard what the Master said: 'I know who betrayed me, but I continue to have faith in them.' Betrayal and faith: two words which seem to be mutually exclusive. How should this assertion be understood when all around us we hear people saying: 'Since I have been betrayed I cannot trust anyone'? The first question to ask yourself is: 'Why does the fact that they have been betrayed make people refuse to trust anyone again?' Quite simply because, in most cases, their trust was not based on respect, admiration, and affection, but on the hope of gaining some advantage from someone. It is a sort of barter based on a calculation: in exchange for trust they will receive certain selfish advantages. Then, of course, when they realize they have been betrayed, they lose their faith, and in losing their faith they lose also their love, because you cannot love someone whose treachery you have discovered. You might as well say that they lose all the beauty and meaning of life.

But when you lose your love for human beings you lose, at the same time, the love of God. This is why Peter Deunov also said: 'If you cannot love human beings, how can you expect God to love you? When you say that you cannot love human beings you make it impossible for God to love you. God loves all his children, and as long as you do not accept that truth you will suffer. Joy is a sign that God loves all human beings; sorrow is a sign that you do not love them. You say: "I love God and the angels, but I cannot love human beings." Well, you must know that you are not reasoning correctly. Henceforth, try to think straight and love all your fellow humans, for the God within you loves them, and if you do not love them you prevent God from loving you.'

Now, even if someone has wronged you greatly you must never say: 'I was mistaken about that person. He has deceived me, he was dishonest, and treacherous, and he is my enemy. I will do everything I can to combat him.' Well, you were mistaken about his character and he injured you in various ways, that is true. But your greatest mistake is in adopting your present attitude, and the injury you do yourself by it will be far greater than anything he did to you. For not only will your negative feelings destroy your own inner harmony, but that person will be lost to you forever. True, he has behaved badly, but if you knew how to react, if you gave him the possibility of recognizing and correcting his faults, he might even become your friend.

Now, I will give you some advice, and one day, if you are capable of following it, you will see the benefits it brings. Suppose you have a colleague whom you trust, who collaborates well, and whom you consider to be a friend. Then, quite by chance, you discover that it was all a sham: he has actually been working against you. Well, if you are sufficiently wise and strong, and if above all you understand the true nature of love, you must not show him that you know that he is disloyal. Be on your guard so as not to be cheated, but continue to behave as a friend, for there is nothing to be gained by trying to settle a score, whereas there is everything to be gained by giving people the opportunity to mend their ways. This law will take effect in spite of you... and in spite of them.

The question is always whether you want to sort out a delicate situation or whether you want to get your own back on someone. Let me give you an example. For many years now married couples have confided in me, and I have seen that one of their most frequent concerns is that of infidelity. Sometimes it is the husband and sometimes the wife who suspects the other of cheating. And sometimes it is not a question of suspicions but of a certitude. And what tragedies result! It is always painful to be betrayed in whatever area, but the pain is even greater when you are betrayed in that most intimate of areas, love. What advice can I give you then? It is, of course, a very difficult question, because nothing and nobody can oblige a man or woman to be faithful to their spouse. But there is no law against trying, and the best way is to create the conditions that would allow your spouse to come back to you.

This is what I have often explained to both men and women. In the case of a woman I tell her: 'I understand that your husband is unfaithful and that this is very painful for you. You could, of course, create a scene: you could cry and scream and tell him that you have found him out; you could threaten him with divorce, or even with suicide. But you must realize that if there is to be any hope of his coming back to you, it is up to you to be intelligent and patient. In the first place, continue to show that you trust him as though you neither knew nor suspected anything. You might even insist on his good qualities; you could tell him how happy you are to have a husband like him to count on, how important that is for the children, and so on.'

Naturally, the woman looks at me in astonishment: how can she attribute to her husband the very virtues that are so lacking in him? It is not possible. So I explain a little more: 'When a woman pretends to believe in the fidelity of her husband, he – knowing full well the truth of the situation – begins to feel very uncomfortable, for when people know themselves to be at fault, an expression of trust is more embarrassing than suspicions and recriminations. Every time he is with his mistress he will think of his wife who believes him to be faithful; her face will come between him and his mistress and make him very uneasy. Later, when he goes home, the warm welcome of his wife will only increase his embarrassment. Her trust and love will touch him deeply, and little by little he will begin to feel torn both ways. Then it will be his mistress who senses that something is wrong and who begins to question him, and if he tells her that he still loves his wife, it will be her turn to create a scene. Finally, after all kinds of ups and downs, the wretched man will go back to his wife who showed so much patience, generosity, and intelligence. Yes, above all intelligence, because true love makes us intelligent. Intelligence does not always produce love, but love, the true kind of love, always produces intelligence. So, there you are, think about all this and try to choose the best attitude.'

Perhaps some of you will think that this tale is too unlikely, that things never happen that way. What do you know about it? There are men and women who have believed me and have used this method, and although, unfortunately, it has not always worked, it has often proved successful. Trust, even feigned trust, can have very beneficial results. You will object that it is a pretence. Well, it depends on what you mean by pretence. I call it educational. It is a question of speaking, without his knowing it, to the noblest aspect of a man's being in order to help him become aware of his duties and responsibilities. There is no question of lying to him, of deceiving or harming him, but on the contrary of providing the conditions that will encourage the manifestation of his true, divine nature. The only problem is that in order to do this, you must have already worked at great length on yourself and achieved considerable self-mastery, otherwise you could too easily give way to instinctive reactions of anger and revolt. You also need to have learned humility.

Unfortunately, humility is not a very common virtue. When they are insulted or wronged, most people would be ashamed not to react immediately:

'Who do you take me for? If you think I'm going to put up with that... I'm not so stupid. You'll see...' Also, many people take pleasure in prying into the private lives of others in the hope of finding some shameful secrets to tell others about. Doubt and distrust are written all over their faces, and their suspicious eyes see nothing but dishonesty and treachery even where they do not exist. Can anyone tell me what advantage there is in behaving like this? Not only do such people sow disorder all around, but they make themselves universally disliked, and their grim expression makes them look like criminals themselves. Yes, that is what is so extraordinary: all these suspicious people end by bearing the signs on their own faces of the faults and vices they keep trying to find in others. Look at the contrast with the faces of those who habitually try to discern people's hidden qualities and virtues: little by little they reflect the light of divine splendor.

By pursuing others with suspicion and distrust you drive them down, and where is the love in that? You should use a little more psychology, a little more educational sense, and try to support them and help them to turn themselves around by showing confidence in them. A lack of trust imprisons people in their faults and failings whereas trust can set them free. When someone behaves badly, even if he has committed a crime, why treat him as though he were bound to keep repeating that crime? His actions belong to the past, and you must not confuse the past and eternity. He has behaved badly, yes, but his misdeeds were situated in a moment in history. He may have changed and mended his ways since then. You must not look only at the past, but at the present and even the future. This is the way of sages and initiates who have a much broader understanding of life: they know that evolution is the law of life and that they themselves once made a great many mistakes before becoming what they are today.

No one becomes a saint or a prophet at the first attempt. You need to have lived through repeated incarnations; you need to have worked and worked, for that is what the earth is: faults, errors, and impurities. How could a Master help and instruct human beings if in his own earlier incarnations he had not experienced the same things and overcome the same difficulties? What virtue would it be in him if he had not endured the same trials in order to become what he is today? He would never dare ask others to make efforts that he himself had not already made. If we need to follow the advice of the initiates and great Masters, it is because they know the way, they know the obstacles that lie along that way, and they know how to overcome them. But what they know above all is that no creature must ever be condemned without appeal, for God works on them and in them.

If I did not believe that the Deity dwells within you, that you yourselves are divinities, I would probably have lost courage and abandoned everything a long time ago. It is for the sake of the Deity within you that I continue my work, and I sometimes adopt an attitude to certain individuals which causes certain of my well-wishers to protest: 'For goodness sake, Master, you welcome this man and treat him trustingly, but surely you have seen what he is? Take care! He is bound to cause trouble.' Yes, I am well aware of what I am doing. It is they who do not understand. I know that thanks to my attitude there is a chance that this person will feel the need to improve. If he does not do so, that is too bad. But I use this pedagogical method consciously, knowing the risks involved. Of course, it is a pity if nothing comes of it, but I will be neither devastated nor discouraged.

We have to give people the best possible conditions so that they may manifest the qualities buried deep – perhaps very deep – within them. We may be surprised by the results – sometimes pleasantly surprised, why should it always turn out badly? But I am neither naïve nor gullible, and when I trust people it is not because I imagine that their egoism will be transformed into generosity, or that their weakness will become strength, and so on. No, I know that that is not possible. The lower nature – you might even say the animal nature – in human beings will not change. But above that nature which expresses itself in egoism, weakness, callousness, deceit, and so on, is another nature which is divine and which is capable of expressing great nobility. I know this nature, and it is to it that I speak, it is to this nature that I send a signal.

If initiates behaved like ordinary people humanity would never have had a chance to evolve. I too have been swindled, deceived, and betrayed to a degree that you could hardly imagine – and in fact it is still going on – but what does that matter? I continue to trust people, even those who may not deserve it. Why? Because I know that it is possible for their divine nature to manifest at the very last minute. This is the true work of a Master.

A Master has meditated for a long time, a very long time, on the love of God and the best way to manifest it. So when he manifests his trust in human beings it is not because he needs them or hopes to gain some advantage for himself by doing so. By trusting them he is giving them a chance... for you never know. But, of course, anyone who uses this method needs to be very strong, because he has to be prepared for the best as well as for the worst. Once you yourselves are strong enough, you will be capable of trusting people without fear of

'As I have loved you'

suffering or being devastated if they betray your trust. In the meantime, keep practising. I tell you these things because I want to share my experience with you, and it is up to you to decide whether or not you want to benefit from it.

The animosity and hatred which human beings feel for each other comes from the fact that when one person is face to face with another neither of them remember that they are in the presence of a spirit, a divine spark which is seeking to express itself, and that it is worth being kind, patient, and generous in order to help it do so. When you realize what people think of each other, what they see in those they encounter, it is not surprising that they end by wanting to kill each other. Even Christians, who for two thousand years have never tired of repeating that we must love each other, continue to live in hatred and discord.

Yes, two thousand years ago Jesus said: *'I give you a new commandment, that you love one another. Just as I have loved you, you also should love one another.'*[15] If we have neither understood nor put this commandment into practice, it is because we have not paid sufficient attention to an essential part of Jesus' message: *'As I have loved you...'* How did he love his disciples? What kind of love was the love of Jesus? What did he see in

---

[15] Jn 13:34-35

human beings? The answer to this is in the Sermon on the Mount when, speaking to his disciples and to the crowds that had followed him, he said: *'Be perfect as your heavenly Father is perfect.'*[16] This means that in his disciples, as in all those who approached him, he saw the image of his heavenly Father, he saw the Deity. And, since he showed them the way of perfection, it was to the Deity within them that he spoke. Other people only saw the miserable outward appearance of those they dismissed as lepers, prostitutes, adulterers, thieves, possessed of the devil, and so on. But Jesus saw in all beings a soul and a spirit which needed only the right conditions to manifest in beauty and light. It was these souls and spirits he loved, it was to them that he spoke.

What is the use of preaching brotherly love if it is never explained what we must love in others and how to love it? The injunction to love one another has been repeated so often without being understood that it has lost all meaning. We are sick and tired of hearing it. When you see the way so many people behave in everyday life it is impossible to love them. It is useless even to try. Here is this selfish, vicious, odious individual... and someone comes along and tells you that you have to love him. It is impossible! It is so

---

[16] Mt 5:48

'As I have loved you'

impossible, indeed, that not only will you fail, but your efforts to love such a monster will make you hate him even more. In order to love him you are going to have to look far beyond appearances and concentrate on the divine spark which dwells within him and which will one day be made manifest. The trouble is, however, that we can recognize the Deity in others only to the extent to which we have learned to bring it to life within ourselves.

Henceforth, if you have understood what I have been saying you will no longer be surprised when I say that I consider men and women to be divinities, and you will try to do the same. In doing this we show our respect for God's work. It is because I admire the wisdom of the Creator that I sense the presence of something infinitely beautiful and precious in every human being, something which deserves to be loved. It does not bother me if my attitude makes some people scoff, thinking that I am living in the midst of illusions. I know that the opposite is true: I am living in true faith based on eternal truths. One of these truths is that God created human beings in his own image. And this means that when we seek the Godhead in each man and each woman, not only are we offering our Creator an expression of our faith and love, but we are also vivifying his presence within ourselves.

By the same author:
(Translated from the French)

Izvor Collection
201 – Toward a Solar Civilization
202 – Man, Master of his Destiny
203 – Education Begins Before Birth
204 – The Yoga of Nutrition
205 – Sexual Force or the Winged Dragon
206 – A Philosophy of Universality
207 – What is a Spiritual Master?
208 – Under the Dove, the Reign of Peace
209 – Christmas and Easter in the Initiatic Tradition
210 – The Tree of the Knowledge of Good and Evil
211 – Freedom, the Spirit Triumphant
212 – Light is a Living Spirit
213 – Man's Two Natures: Human and Divine
214 – Hope for the World: Spiritual Galvanoplasty
215 – The True Meaning of Christ's Teaching
216 – The Living Book of Nature
217 – New Light on the Gospels
218 – The Symbolic Language of Geometrical Figures
219 – Man's Subtle Bodies and Centres
220 – The Zodiac, Key to Man and to the Universe
221 – True Alchemy or the Quest for Perfection
222 – Man's Psychic Life: Elements and Structures
223 – Creation: Artistic and Spiritual
224 – The Powers of Thought
225 – Harmony and Health
226 – The Book of Divine Magic
227 – Golden Rules for Everyday Life
228 – Looking into the Invisible
229 – The Path of Silence
230 – The Book of Revelations: a Commentary
231 – The Seeds of Happiness
232 – The Mysteries of Fire and Water
233 – Youth: Creators of the Future
234 – Truth, Fruit of Wisdom and Love
235 – 'In Spirit and in Truth'
236 – Angels and other Mysteries of The Tree of Life
237 – Cosmic Balance, The Secret of Polarity
238 – The Faith That Moves Mountains
239 – Love Greater Than Faith

Books by Omraam Mikhaël Aïvanhov
(translated from the French)

Complete Works

Volume 1 – The Second Birth
Volume 2 – Spiritual Alchemy
Volume 5 – Life Force
Volume 6 – Harmony
Volume 7 – The Mysteries of Yesod
Volume 10 – The Splendour of Tiphareth
　　　　　　　The Yoga of the Sun
Volume 11 – The Key to the Problems of Existence
Volume 12 – Cosmic Moral Laws
Volume 13 – A New Earth
　　　　　　　Methods, Exercises, Formulas, Prayers
Volume 14 – Love and Sexuality (Part I)
Volume 15 – Love and Sexuality (Part II)
Volume 17 – 'Know Thyself' Jnana Yoga (Part I)
Volume 18 – 'Know Thyself' Jnana Yoga (Part II)
Volume 25 – A New Dawn:
　　　　　　　Society and Politics in the Light of Initiatic Science (Part I)
Volume 26 – A New Dawn:
　　　　　　　Society and Politics in the Light of Initiatic Science (Part II)
Volume 29 – On the Art of Teaching (Part III)
Volume 30 – Life and Work in an Initiatic School
　　　　　　　Training for the Divine
Volume 32 – The Fruits of the Tree of Life
　　　　　　　The Cabbalistic Tradition

Brochures:

301 – The New Year
302 – Meditation
303 – Respiration
304 – Death and the Life Beyond

By the same author:

Daily Meditations:
A thought for each day of the year
A volume published every year

Life Recordings on Tape
KC2510 AN – The Laws of Reincarnation
              (Two audio cassettes)

Videos (french/english)

V 4605 FR – *The Activity of the Soul and Spirit:*
             How They Can Manifest Through Us.
             How Can We Modify our Destiny?
             L'activité de l'âme et de l'esprit et notre travail
             pour qu'ils se manifestent à travers nous.
             Comment peut-on changer sa destinée?

V 4606 FR – *How Can We Purify our Physical Body*
             Despite the Pollution of the Atmosphere and Food?
             Comment peut-on purifier le corps physique
             malgré la pollution de l'air et de la nourriture?

World Wide - Editor-Distributor
Editions PROSVETA S.A. - B.P. 12 - F- 83601 Fréjus Cedex (France)
Tel. (00 33) 04 94 40 82 41 - Fax (00 33) 04 94 40 80 05
Web: **www.prosveta.com**
e-mail: **international@prosveta.com**

Distributors

AUSTRALIA & NEW ZEALAND
SURYOMA LTD - P.O. Box 2218 – Bowral – N.S.W. 2576
e-mail: info@suryoma.com - Tel. (61) 2 4872 3999 – fax (61) 2 4872 4022

AUSTRIA
HARMONIEQUELL VERSAND – A- 5302 Henndorf am Wallersee, Hof 37
Tel. / fax (43) 6214 7413 – e-mail: info@prosveta.at

BELGIUM & LUXEMBOURG
PROSVETA BENELUX – Liersesteenweg 154 B-2547 Lint
Tel (32) 3/455 41 75 – Fax 3/454 24 25 – e-mail: prosveta@skynet.be
N.V. MAKLU Somersstraat 13-15 – B-2000 Antwerpen
Tel. (32) 3/231 29 00 – Fax 3/233 26 59
VANDER S.A. – Av. des Volontaires 321 – B-1150 Bruxelles
Tel. (32) 27 62 98 00 – Fax 27 62 06 62

BULGARIA
SVETOGLED – Bd Saborny 16 A, appt 11 – 9000 Varna
e-mail: svetgled@revolta.com – Tel/Fax: (359) 52 23 98 02

CANADA
PROSVETA Inc. – 3950, Albert Mines – North Hatley (Qc), J0B 2C0
Tel. (819) 564-8212 – Fax. (819) 564-1823
in Canada, call toll free: 1-800-854-8212
e-mail: prosveta@prosveta-canada.com / www.prosveta-canada.com

COLUMBIA
PROSVETA – Calle 146 # 25-28 Aptp 404 Int.2 – Bogotá
e-mail: kalagiya@tutopia.com

CYPRUS
THE SOLAR CIVILISATION BOOKSHOP – BOOKBINDING
73 D Kallipoleos Avenue - Lycavitos – P. O. Box 24947, 1355 – Nicosia
Tel / Fax 00357-2-377503

CZECH REPUBLIC
PROSVETA – Ant. Sovy 18, –České Budejovice 370 05
Tel / Fax: (420) 38-53 00 227 – e-mail: prosveta@iol.cz

GERMANY
PROSVETA Deutschland – Postfach 16 52 – 78616 Rottweil
Tel. (49) 741-46551 – Fax. (49) 741-46552 – e-mail: prosveta.de@t-online.de
EDIS GmbH, Mühlweg 2 – 82054 Sauerlach
Tel. (49) 8104-6677-0 – Fax.(49) 8104-6677-99

GREAT BRITAIN – IRELAND
PROSVETA – The Doves Nest, Duddleswell Uckfield, – East Sussex TN 22 3JJ
Tel. (44) (01825) 712988 - Fax (44) (01825) 713386
e-mail: prosveta@pavilion.co.uk

GREECE
  PROSVETA – J. Vamvacas
  Moutsopoulou 103 – 18541 Piraeus
HAITI
  PROSVETA – DÉPÔT – B.P. 115, Jacmel, Haiti (W.I.)
  Tel./ Fax (509) 288-3319
  e-mail: uwbhaiti@citeweb.net
HOLLAND
  STICHTING PROSVETA NEDERLAND
  Zeestraat 50 – 2042 LC Zandvoort – e-mail: prosveta@worldonline.nl
ISRAEL
  Zohar, P. B. 1046, Netanya 42110
  e-mail: zohar@wanadoo.fr
ITALY
  PROSVETA Coop. – Casella Postale – 06060 Moiano (PG)
  Tel. (39) 075-8358498 – Fax 075-8359712
  e-mail: prosveta@tin.it
NORWAY
  PROSVETA NORDEN – Postboks 5101 – 1503 Moss
  Tel. (47) 69 26 51 40 – Fax (47) 69 25 06 76
  e-mail: prosveta Norden - prosnor@online.no
PORTUGAL & BRAZIL
  EDIÇÕES PROSVETA – Rua Passos Manuel, n° 20 – 3e E, P 1150 – Lisboa
  Tel. (351) (21) 354 07 64
  PUBLICAÇÕES EUROPA-AMERICA Ltd
  Est Lisboa-Sintra KM 14 – 2726 Mem Martins Codex
  e-mail : prosvetapt@hotmail.com
ROMANIA
  ANTAR – Str. N. Constantinescu 10 - Bloc 16A - sc A - Apt. 9,
  Sector 1 – 71253 Bucarest
  Tel. (40) 1 679 52 48 - Tel./ Fax (40) 1 231 37 19
  e-mail : antared@pcnet.ro
RUSSIA
  EDITIONS PROSVETA S.a.r.l
  Riazanski Prospekt 8a, office 407 – 109428 Moscou
  Tel / Fax (7095) 232 08 79 – e-mail : prosveta@online.ru
SPAIN
  ASOCIACIÓN PROSVETA ESPAÑOLA – C/ Ausias March n° 23 Ático
  SP-08010 Barcelona – Tel (34) (3) 412 31 85 - Fax (34) (3) 302 13 72
  aprosveta@prosveta.es
SWITZERLAND
  PROSVETA Société Coopérative – CH - 1808 Les Monts-de-Corsier
  Tel. (41) 21 921 92 18 – Fax. (41) 21 922 92 04
  e-mail: prosveta@swissonline.ch
UNITED STATES
  PROSVETA U.S.A. – P.O. Box 1176 – New Smyrna Beach, FL.32170-1176
  Tel / Fax (386) 428-1465
  e-mail: sales@prosveta-usa.com – web page: www.prosveta-usa.com
VENEZUELA
  BETTY MUNÖZ – Las Mercedes, Calle Madrid – Quinta Monteserino – D. F. Caracas
  Tel. (58) 0414 22 36 748 – e-mail : miguelclavijo@hotmail.com

Achevé d'imprimer en Octobre 2001
sur les presses de l'Imprimerie HEMISUD
83160 – La Valette-du-Var